101 Employer And Employee Tax Secrets Revealed

2013/14

By

Sarah Bradford

TAX INSIDER
How to beat the taxman and boost your income

Publisher Details

This guide is published by Tax Insider Ltd, 3 Sanderson Close, Great Sankey, Warrington WA5 3LN.

'101 Employer and Employee Tax Secrets Revealed' was first published in September 2013.

A CIP Copy of this book is available from the British Library.

ISBN 978-0-9576139-4-2

Disclaimer

1. This guide is produced for general guidance only, and professional advice should be sought before any decision is made. Individual circumstances can vary and therefore no responsibility can be accepted by Tax Insider, the co-author Sarah Bradford, or the publisher Tax Insider Ltd for any action taken or any decision made to refrain from action by any readers of this guide.

2. Tax rules and legislation are constantly changing and therefore the information printed in this guide is correct at the time of writing — August 2013.

3. Neither the authors nor Tax Insider Ltd offer financial, legal or investment advice. If you require such advice then we urge you to seek the opinion of an appropriate professional in the relevant field. We care about your success and therefore encourage you to take appropriate advice before you put any of your financial or other resources at risk. Don't forget, investment values can decrease as well as increase.

4. The content of this guide is for information only and all examples and numbers are for illustration. Professional advice should always be sought before undertaking any tax planning of any sort as individual circumstances vary and other considerations may have to be taken into account before acting.

5. To the fullest extent permitted by law Sarah Bradford and Tax Insider Ltd do not accept liability for any direct, indirect, special, consequential or other losses or damages of whatsoever kind arising from using this guide.

The guide itself is provided 'as is' without express or implied warranty.

Publisher Details

This guide is published by [illegible]

[illegible] Employed and Employed Tax Secrets Revealed was first published in [illegible]

A CIP Copy of this book is available from the British Library.

ISBN 978-0-9576139-4-2

Contents

Chapter 4. Family And Welfare Benefits

Chapter 5. Other Popular Benefits

Chapter 6. Termination Of Employment

About This Guide

The opportunities for employees to legitimately reduce the tax that they pay are more limited than for the self-employed and those operating through a family company. However, the tax legislation includes a surprisingly large number of exemptions and reliefs which make it possible for employers to implement tax-efficient remuneration strategies and to provide elements of the remuneration package free of tax.

This guide contains 101 Tax Tips for Employees and Employers. It highlights various exemptions and reliefs available to employees, methods for saving work and strategies for tax-efficient remuneration.

However, it should be noted that tips in this guide are for illustration purposes only and are intended to demonstrate where tax savings can be made. The savings that can be made will depend on the precise circumstances and the examples are a guide only. Professional advice should always be sought.

Chapter 1.
Tax-Efficient Remuneration

1. Designing A Tax-Efficient Remuneration Package
2. Making Use Of Salary-Sacrifice Arrangements
3. Consider A Flexible Benefits System
4. Choose Non-Cash Benefits To Save Employee NICs
5. Provide Benefits To P9D Employees Tax-Free
6. The £8,500 Trap

1. Designing A Tax-Efficient Remuneration Package

A typical remuneration package comprises a number of elements. Some of these are subject to legislative control. For example, employers must comply with National Minimum Wage legislation, equal pay legislation and provide paid holiday at least equal to the statutory minimum. However, other aspects of the remuneration package are at the discretion of the employer.

In setting the remuneration package, the employer must have regard to a range of factors, including the culture of the organisation, market conditions and industry norms. However, within these parameters there are opportunities to structure the package to take advantage of the various tax and National Insurance exemptions and reliefs available. These can generate tax and National Insurance savings for the employee and National Insurance savings for the employer.

The opportunity to save tax and National Insurance should be taken into account when designing a remuneration package.

2. Making Use Of Salary Sacrifice Arrangements

A salary sacrifice scheme allows the employer to offer employees the opportunity to benefit from the tax exemptions available for a range of benefits in kind, without passing the cost of providing those benefits to the employer.

Under a salary sacrifice scheme, the employee gives up a certain amount of cash salary in return for a non-cash benefit. Usually the benefit taken in exchange for the salary is one for which a tax exemption is available. However, the scheme can also be used in relation to taxable benefits to take advantage of the National Insurance savings available to the employee by replacing cash salary which is liable to employee and employer Class 1 contributions with a non-cash benefit which is liable to employer-only Class 1A contributions.

Where an employee swaps cash salary for a tax-exempt benefit, the employee will save tax and employee Class 1 National Insurance contributions and the employer will save employer Class 1 National Insurance contributions. Salary sacrifice arrangements are often used to enable the employee to benefit from the tax exemption for childcare vouchers.

To be effective, the employee must not be able to revert to the higher salary at will. Care must also be taken where the employee earns near the National Minimum Wage (NMW) as the salary sacrifice cannot reduce cash earnings below the NMW. Reducing cash salary below the lower earnings limit for Class 1 National Insurance purposes (£109 per week for 2013/14) may adversely affect entitlement to the state pension, contributory benefits and statutory payments.

Making Use Of Salary Sacrifice Arrangements

Helen's employer operates a salary sacrifice scheme to enable employees to swap cash salary for non-cash benefits. Helen takes advantage of the scheme by giving up £2,860 of cash salary for childcare vouchers.

Helen is a basic rate taxpayer and as such is able to enjoy the benefit of childcare vouchers of up to £55 per week free of tax and National Insurance.

By swapping cash salary, which is subject to tax and National Insurance, for a tax and National Insurance free benefit, Helen saves tax of £572 (£2,860 @ 20%) and National Insurance of £343.20. She is therefore £915.20 a year better off.

Helen's employer also benefits, saving employer Class 1 National Insurance of £394.68 on the foregone salary.

By using a salary sacrifice arrangement to swap cash salary for an exempt benefit everyone wins.

3. Consider A Flexible Benefits System

Happy employees are generally more productive than disgruntled employees. Operating a flexible benefits system enables employees to tailor their remuneration package to suit their individual circumstances and preferences. Certain elements of the package must be fixed, such as a minimum level of cash salary, holiday and pension provision, but the employee is given a certain amount, either in the form of pounds or points, which can be taken in the form of salary or benefits.

By choosing exempt benefits, the employee can save tax and National Insurance and the employer can save employer Class 1 National Insurance.

Consider A Flexible Benefits System

Bill and Ben work for the same company. Their employer operates a flexible benefits package. Both are entitled to a salary of £40,000 and have 100 points which can be spent on additional salary or on a variety of benefits.

Bill chooses to spend his 100 points on additional salary of £10,000 a year.

Ben chooses a company car (50 points), private medical insurance (5 points), an additional two weeks holiday (20 points) and additional cash salary of £2,500 (25 points).

The system allows Bill and Ben to tailor their package to their individual requirements.

4. Choose Non-Cash Benefits To Save Employee NICs

Even if a benefit is not exempt from tax and National Insurance, it can still be beneficial from the employee's perspective to choose the benefit rather than cash salary as this will save employee Class 1 National Insurance contributions.

Most taxable benefits provided to employees earning at a rate of at least £8,500 a year or to directors, are liable to Class 1A National Insurance contributions rather than to Class 1. Class 1A National Insurance is only payable by the employer – there are no employee Class 1A contributions.

By swapping cash salary for a non-cash benefit, the National Insurance liability switches from Class 1 (payable by both employees and employers) to Class 1A (employer only) saving employee National Insurance contributions.

If the employee earns at a rate of less than £8,500 (a P9D employee), the employer will also escape National Insurance contributions as Class 1A National Insurance is not payable on benefits provided to P9D employees, even if those benefits are taxable.

Choose Non-Cash Benefits To Save Employee NICs

George receives a cash salary of £30,000 a year and private medical insurance of £600 a year. He pays no National Insurance on the private medical insurance. As a result he is £72 per year better off than if he had received an additional £600 in salary and paid for the medical insurance from his net pay.

The employer pays Class 1A National Insurance of £82.80 on the benefit – which is the same as the employer Class 1 contributions payable on salary of £600. Although the employer is not better off, the employer enjoys a cash-flow advantage as Class 1A contributions are paid after the end of the tax year whereas Class 1 contributions are payable during the year.

5. Provide Benefits To P9D Employees Tax-Free

The vast majority of non-cash benefits are only taxable when provided to employees earning at a rate of more than £8,500 a year (P11D employees) and to directors. P9D employees are only taxed on benefits in money or money's worth (such as those which can be converted to cash by sale or surrender) or which are taxable on all employees, such as living accommodation. This provides the opportunity to provide P9D employees with tax-free benefits. This can be useful in a small family company where an employee only works maybe one day a week.

However, in working out whether an employee is a P9D employee earning at a rate of less than £8,500 a year it is necessary to take into account the cash equivalent value of any benefits provided.

Provide Benefits To P9D Employees

Lucy works six hours a week, earning a salary of £3,120 a year. As her job involves making deliveries, she also has a company car with a cash equivalent value of £4,000.

Lucy earns at the rate of £7,120 a year (cash salary of £3,120 plus benefits in kind of £4,000). As her earnings rate is below £8,500 she is not taxed on the provision of her company car as the benefit of a company car is only taxable on P11D employees and directors.

The car is provided to Lucy tax-free. Further, there is no Class 1A National Insurance liability on her employer.

6. The £8,500 Trap

As explained in Tip 5, most benefits in kind are only taxable when provided to P11D employees (employees earnings at a rate of at least £8,500 a year) and to directors regardless of their earnings level. A lower paid (P9D) employee is one who earns at a rate of less than £8,500 a year.

However, an employee whose actual cash salary is less than £8,500 in a tax year can still be regarded as earning at a rate of more than £8,500 a year for the purposes of the benefits in kind legislation.

This is because the cash equivalent value of benefits in kind is taken into account in working out whether the £8,500 threshold has been reached. Further, where the employee is only employed for part of the tax year, the annualised earnings are used to ascertain whether the threshold has been reached, rather than actual earnings for the period of the employment.

However, if an employee works part-time, it is the part-time salary that is used to ascertain the earnings rate rather than the full-time equivalent salary.

The £8,500 Trap

Polly works part time and earns £6,000 a year. She does not receive any benefits in kind. She earns at the rate of £6,000 a year and is a lower paid (P9D) employee.

Alice starts work on 6 October 2013. In the six months from 6 October 2013 to 5 April 2014 she earns £6,000. However, as she only works for part of the year, her annualised earnings (£6,000/6 x 12) are used to determine her earnings rate. She therefore earns at the rate of £12,000 a year and is not a lower paid (P9D) employee.

Emily also works part time and earns £6,000 a year. She also has a company car with a cash equivalent value of £3,000. As the cash equivalent value of the car is taken into account in determining her earnings rate, she is not a lower paid (P9D) employee. Consequently, she is taxed on the benefit of the company car.

Chapter 2.
Travel, Transport And Meals

7. Tax-Free Mileage Allowance Payments

The Approved Mileage Allowance Payments (AMAPs) scheme allows employers to pay tax-free mileage allowances to employees who use their own cars for business journeys, as long as the allowance paid does not exceed the approved amount.

Any amounts paid in excess of the approved amount are taxable and must be notified to HMRC on the employee's P11D.

The approved amount is found by the formula

$$M \times R$$

Where:

- *M* is the number of miles of business travel by the employee (other than as a passenger) using that kind of vehicle in the tax year in question; and
- *R* is the rate applicable to that kind of vehicle.

For 2013/14 the rates are as follows:

Cars and vans	45p per mile for the first 10,000 business miles
	25p per mile after that
Motor cycles	24p per mile
Cycles	20p per mile

Tax-Free Mileage Allowance Payments

Mark's employer pays a mileage allowance of 40p per mile.

During 2013/14 Mark drives 12,000 business miles in his own car.

Mark's employer pays him a mileage allowance of £4,800.

The approved amount is £5,000 (being 10,000 miles @ 45p per mile (£4,500) plus 2,000 miles @ 25p per mile (£500).

As the amount paid is less than the approved amount the allowance is paid free of tax and there is nothing to report to HMRC on Mark's P11D.

8. Mileage Allowance Relief

Where an employer does not pay a mileage allowance to an employee who uses his or her own car for work or pays an allowance which is less than the approved amount, the employee can claim tax relief for the shortfall. This can be done in the employee's self-assessment return, on form P87 or by writing to HMRC.

Mileage Allowance Relief

Gillian uses her car for work. Her employer pays her a mileage allowance of 30p per mile. In 2013/14 she drove 9,000 business miles in her own car.

Gillian received mileage allowances of £2,700 (9,000 miles @ 30p per mile) from her employer for using her car for business.

The approved amount is £4,050 (9,000 miles @ 45p per mile).

Gillian can claim tax relief for the shortfall of £1,350.

If she is a basic rate taxpayer, this is worth £270 (£1,350 @ 20%). If she is a higher rate taxpayer, it is worth £540.

9. NIC-Free Mileage Allowance Payments

Employers can also pay mileage allowance payments free of National Insurance contributions as long as the amount paid does not exceed the approved amount. The mileage allowance scheme for National Insurance purposes is similar to that applying for tax purposes (see Tip 7), but with one key difference – the rate for cars and vans is 45p per mile regardless of the number of business miles driven. This is because unlike tax, National Insurance contributions are computed separately for each earnings period rather than cumulatively.

NIC-Free Mileage Allowance Payments

Jessica uses her car for business and is paid a mileage allowance of 45p per mile. She drives 15,000 miles in the tax year.

No NIC liability arises in respect of the allowance as it is paid at the approved rate for NIC purposes of 45p per mile.

However, a tax liability will arise as the allowance paid exceeds the approved amount for tax purposes (see Tip 7).

10. Tax-Free Passenger Payments

Employers can also pay a tax-free allowance to employees who give lifts to passengers for whom the journey is also a business journey.

The approved amount is found by the formula

$M \times R$

Where:

- *M* is the number if miles of business travel by the employee by car or van for which the employee carries one or more passenger for whom the travel is business travel and in respect of whom passenger payments are made; and
- *R* is the rate of 5p per mile.

Any passenger payments made in excess of the approved amount are taxable and must be returned on the employee's P11D.

However, if the employer does not make passenger payments or makes them at a rate less than the approved amount, the employee is not able to claim tax relief for the shortfall.

Tax-Free Passenger Payments

Joe frequently uses his car for business journeys. His employer encourages car sharing.

In 2013/14 he gave lifts to Matt in respect of journeys totalling 3,000 business miles, to Ellie in respect of business journeys totalling 570 business miles and to Kalim in respect of business journeys totalling 2,400 business miles.

Joe's employer can make tax-free passenger payments of £150 (3,000 miles @ 5p per mile) in respect of the lifts given to Matt, £28.50 (570 @ 5p per mile) in respect of the lifts given to Ellie and £120 (2,400 miles @ 5p per mile) in respect of the lifts given to Kalim – a total tax-free payment of £298.50.

From the employer's perspective it is much cheaper to encourage car-sharing and to pay passenger payments of 5p per mile than for each employee to take their own car and for the employer to make mileage payments of 45p per mile.

11. Advisory Fuel Rates

The Approved Mileage Allowance Payments system only applies where an employee uses his or her own car for business journeys. It does not apply where the employee has a company car.

However, HMRC publish advisory fuel rates, which can be used to negotiate dispensations in respect of mileage payments made to company car drivers using their car for business journeys. The rates are not tax-free rates. However, where a dispensation is in force, the employer does not need to report the payments to HMRC and the employee is relieved from the need to claim any corresponding tax relief.

The rates can also be used to determine the amount that the employee must reimburse in respect of private travel in a case where an employee is provided with fuel for travel in a company car but must make good the cost of the fuel used for private journeys in order to prevent a fuel benefit charge arising.

The advisory fuel rates applying from 1 September 2013 are as follows:

Engine Size	Petrol	LPG
1,400cc or less	15p per mile	10p per mile
1,401cc to 2,000cc	18p per mile	11p per mile
Over 2,000cc	26p per mile	16p per mile

Engine Size	Diesel
1,600cc or less	12p per mile
1,601cc to 2,000cc	15p per mile
Over 2,000cc	18p per mile

Advisory Fuel Rates

Harry has a company car. His employer does not provide fuel.

Harry uses his car for business. His employer pays Harry a mileage allowance in accordance with the advisory fuel rates. Harry has a 1,600cc petrol car and in accordance with the rates applying from 1 September 2013 receives 18p per mile for business journeys in his company car.

Harry's employer has a dispensation in force drawn-up in terms of the advisory rates.

As long as the amount paid to employee does not exceed the advisory rate, Harry's employer does not need to return details of the payments to HMRC and Harry does not need to claim tax relief. The payments are effectively made tax-free.

12. Workplace Parking

Parking costs can be high, particularly in city centre locations. As such the provision of a parking space at or near the employee's place of work can be a valuable benefit.

No tax charge arises where the employer provides workplace parking for an employee or where the employer reimburses expenses incurred by the employee in connection with the provision of or the use by the employee of workplace parking.

Workplace parking means a parking space for a car or van, a motorcycle parking space or facilities for parking a cycle other than a motor cycle at or near the employee's workplace. HMRC allow the exemption for parking facilities within reasonable distance of the workplace. This means that the provision does not need to be in the nearest car park to the workplace.

Workplace Parking

Robert's employer rents car parking spaces in a car park near to the office for use by employees. Employees can park free of charge.

Robert is allocated a parking space.

There is no tax charge in respect of benefit of the parking space.

The provision of the parking space saves Robert £1,200 a year in parking charges.

13. Employer-Provided Cycles

To encourage employees to cycle to work, employers can loan employees cycles and/or cycling safety equipment without triggering a benefits in kind tax charge provided that the following conditions are met:

- there is no transfer of property in the cycle or any equipment provided;
- the employee uses the cycle or equipment mainly for qualifying journeys; and
- the cycles and/or equipment are made available to employees generally.

A qualifying journey is a journey between home and work or between two workplaces. This exemption allows the employer to meet the cost of the employee's journey to work tax-free.

The exemption can be used in conjunction with salary sacrifice arrangements (see Tip 2) as part of a cycle to work scheme.

No tax charge arises on any subsequent transfer of ownership to the employee provided that the employee pays at least the market value of the cycle. HMRC allow a simplified approach to be used for valuing cycles at a percentage of their original value depending on their age at the time of disposal (see HMRC's Employment Income Manual at EIM21667a).

Employer-Provided Cycles

Imran's employer is keen to encourage employees to cycle to work and to enjoy the associated health and environmental benefits.

Under the cycle to work scheme, employees can borrow a cycle and helmet from the employer for a period of two years.

At the end of the loan period, the employee can either return the cycle to the employer or buy it for its current market value.

As the conditions of the exemption are met, Imran can enjoy the use of the cycle tax-free.

Further, no tax charge arises on the transfer of ownership at the end of the loan period as Imran has paid the market value.

14. Works Bus Services

Normally a tax charge arises where an employer meets the costs of an employee's travel from home to work. However, an employer can provide tax-free home to work travel for employees by means of a works transport service, as long as the conditions attaching to the exemption are met.

For the exemption to apply, the service must be generally available to the employees of the employer or employers concerned, the main use of the service must be for qualifying journeys and the service must be used only or mainly by the employees for whom it is provided and their children.

Qualifying journeys are journeys between the employee's home and work or between two workplaces. However, the bus can also be used for short trips, such as to the shops at lunchtime, without jeopardising the exemption as long as the non-qualifying journey is not more than ten miles and is made on a work day.

The service must be provided by a bus (seat capacity of at least 12) or a minibus (9, 10 or 11 seats). A people carrier cannot be used.

Works Bus Service

Jan works at a biscuit factory. His employer operates a works bus service which Jan uses to travel to and from work. No tax charge arises in respect of the use of the service.

15. Subsidised Public Bus Services

Running a works bus service (see Tip 14) is expensive and may be beyond the means of many employers. However, employers can still provide home to work bus travel for employees, either free or at a reduced cost, without triggering a tax charge by subsidising a public bus service.

If the service is a local bus service, for the exemption to apply the service must be used by the employees for qualifying journeys and the opportunity to use the service must be available to the employer's employees generally. Qualifying journeys are home to work journeys and journeys between two workplaces.

If the subsidised service is not a local service, the terms on which the service is available to the employees must not be more favourable than those available to other passengers for the exemption to apply.

The support can be financial support or other support, such as arranging for a bus shelter to be built.

Subsidised Public Bus Service

Molly works on a small industrial estate. Her employer, together with other employers on the industrial estate, provides financial support for a local bus service in return for the service stopping at the industrial estate and providing discounted travel for employees.

Molly uses the service to travel to and from work.

No tax charge arises in respect of the support provided by her employer or the discounted travel.

16. Late Night Taxis

Occasionally employees may be required to work late, for example to meet a tight deadline. As a measure of goodwill, the employer may provide a taxi home where an employee works unusually late.

The normal rule is that a taxable benefit arises wherever the employer meets the cost of home to work travel. However, an employer can provide a taxi home without triggering a tax charge as long as all of the four late working conditions are met.

These are that:

- the employee is required to work later than usual until at least 9pm;
- this occurs irregularly;
- by the time that the employee ceases work, public transport has ceased to be available to the employee or it would not be reasonable to expect the employee to use it (e.g. due to safety concerns); and
- the transport is provided by taxi or similar private road transport.

A taxi home can also be provided tax-free where an employee normally comes to work with another employee under car-sharing arrangements and those arrangements fail due to unforeseen circumstances (such as the driver leaving early to collect a sick child).

Tax-free taxis home cannot be provided on more than 60 occasions in the tax year.

Late Night Taxis

Jack works for a bakery, which specialises in wedding and celebration cakes. He normally finishes work at 6pm. However, in order to meet a last-minute order for a birthday cake, he works until 10pm. The normal bus he takes home stops running at 9.30pm, so his employer provides a taxi for him.

As the conditions for exemption are met, the provision of the taxi is free of tax.

17. Incidental Overnight Expenses

Employers can take advantage of the exemption for incidental overnight expenses to pay an allowance to employees who are required to stay away from home overnight on business. The allowance is designed to cover incidental costs of staying away such as newspapers, laundry and phoning home.

The allowance is set at £5 per night for stays in the UK and £10 per night for stays abroad. However, if these limits are exceeded, the full amount paid to the employee (not just the excess over £5 or £10 as applicable) is subject to tax and National Insurance.

Incidental Overnight Expenses

Ben attends a sales conference in France and stays away from home for three nights. His employer pays him an allowance of £30 tax-free to cover incidental overnight expenses.

18. Benchmark Advisory Rates For Subsistence Payments

To save work, consider negotiating dispensations with HMRC for subsistence by reference to scale rates. An easy option is to use the advisory benchmark scale rates set by HMRC.

The rates are set out in HMRC's Employment Income Manual at EIM05231 as follows:

Breakfast rate	£5
One-meal (5 hour) rate	£5
Two-meal (10 hour) rate	£10
Late evening meal rate	£15

The benchmark rates are the maximum amounts that can be paid tax free. Payments in excess of these rates which are not agreed with HMRC may be liable to tax and National Insurance.

Separate rates apply to employees subject to working rule agreements.

Benchmark Advisory Rates For Subsistence Payments.

Neil visits a supplier as part of the duties of his employment. He leaves home at 5am, two hours earlier than usual and returns at 7pm. His employer has agreed a dispensation with HMRC based on their advisory benchmark rates.

Neil is paid subsistence expenses of £15, being the breakfast rate of £5 and the two-meal (10 hour) rate of £10.

19. Tea And Coffee

Although there is a separate exemption for subsidised meals (see Tip 20), where this exemption does not apply, for example because provision is not available to all employees, HMRC will not seek tax on the provision of free tea and coffee or water from a water dispenser as they regard it as a trivial benefit.

Tea And Coffee

Some of the workers of ABC Ltd are based on the road, others are office based. Employees who are based in the office are able to enjoy free tea and coffee. This privilege is not available to travelling employees.

Despite the fact that all employees are not able to benefit from the provision of free tea and coffee, no tax charge arises in respect of its provision as it is exempt as a trivial benefit.

20. Workplace Canteens

Employers are able to provide free and subsidised meals for employees free of tax as long as:

- the meal is on a reasonable scale;
- all employees, or all the employees at a particular location, may obtain either a free or subsidised meal or a voucher to obtain such a meal; and
- in the case of hotel, catering or similar business, if the meals are provided to employees in a restaurant or dining room used by members of the public, part of the room must be designated for staff use and employees must take their meals there.

All employees must be able to benefit from a meal but they do not all need to have the same meal or eat in the same room. Nor does the canteen have to be on the employer's premises for the exemption to apply.

Beware of using salary sacrifice arrangements (see Tip 2) to take advantage of the exemption because it no longer applies where free or cheap meals are provided as part of a salary sacrifice or flexible remuneration arrangement.

Workplace Canteens

John works at a large engineering works. All employees are able to benefit from subsidised meals in the staff canteen. There is a separate canteen for directors.

The exemption applies and no taxable benefit arises from the provision of subsidised meals.

21. Beware The 'Sandwich Working Lunch' Trap

Meetings often run on and when they run over lunchtime the employer may provide a sandwich lunch as a gesture of goodwill. Many employers would not even think about the possible tax consequences of such a gesture, but that would be misguided.

The exemption for subsidised meals (see Tip 20) does not apply as meals are not made available for all employees. Consequently a tax charge will arise on the benefit.

Most employers do not want employees to be taxed on the provision of the occasional sandwich. Consequently, it is advisable to settle the liability by means of a PAYE Settlement Agreement.

The tax implications of sandwich lunches are easily overlooked. HMRC know this and it is often something they look for in a PAYE visit.

Beware The 'Sandwich Working Lunch' Trap

Mike runs a small company with 20 employees. Where a meeting runs through lunch, he will often order in a sandwich lunch for the employees in the meeting. As lunch is not provided for all employees, the benefit of the lunch is not tax-free.

Mike's accountant suggests he agrees a PAYE Settlement Agreement with HMRC to settle the liability on his employees' behalf. This he does, enabling the employees to enjoy their lunch without receiving a tax bill for dessert.

Chapter 3.
Cars, Vans And Other Vehicles

22. Choose A Car With Lower Emissions
23. Choose A Very Low Emission Car For A 5% Charge
24. Choose A Cheaper Car
25. List Price Versus Price Actually Paid
26. Limit Optional Accessories
27. Drive An Electric Company Car Tax-Free
28. Tax-Free Company Cars For Lower Paid Employees
29. Cars For Family Members
30. Limit Capital Contributions To £5,000
31. Private Use Contributions
32. Periods Of Unavailability Of Less Than 30 Days
33. Beware Superior Replacements
34. Cash Alternative To A Company Car
35. Planning Ahead For Future Tax Changes
36. Free Fuel – A Worthwhile Benefit?
37. Impact Of Car Choice On Fuel Benefit
38. Free Fuel – A More Expensive Benefit Than A Company Car?
39. Making Good The Cost Of Private Fuel
40. Avoid Partial Reimbursement
41. Making Good – Beware The Timing Trap
42. Withdrawing Provision Of Free Fuel

22. Choose A Car With Lower Emissions

Despite high tax charges, company car remains a popular benefit. Where a company car is made available for the private use of an employee earning at a rate of at least £8,500 a year (a P11D employee) or a director irrespective of his or her earnings level, a taxable benefit arises.

The amount charged to tax is the cash equivalent of the benefit.

The main determinants of the cash equivalent are the price of the car and its CO_2 emissions. The level of CO_2 emissions determines the percentage of the car's price which is charged to tax.

HMRC reward those who make green choices with a lower tax charge. Therefore, to minimise the tax charge on a company car, choose one with low emissions.

Choose A Car With Lower Emissions

Under their company car policy, Penny and Nick are each able to choose a car with a list price of £20,000.

Penny chooses a car with CO_2 emissions of 120g/km. The appropriate percentage for 2013/14 for a car with CO_2 emissions of 120g/km is 16%. Therefore the cash equivalent value of the car is £3,200. Assuming Penny is a higher rate taxpayer, she will pay tax of £1,280 on the benefit of her company car for 2013/14.

Nick chooses a high performance model with CO_2 emissions of 200g/km. For 2013/14 the cash equivalent value for a car with CO_2 emissions of 200g/km is 32%. This equates to a cash equivalent value of £6,400. Assuming Nick is also a higher rate taxpayer, he will pay tax of £2,560 on the benefit of his car for 2013/14.

By choosing a high emission model, Nick pays twice as much tax as Penny, even though their cars have the same list price.

23. Choose A Very Low Emission Car For A 5% Charge

For five years from 6 April 2010 until 5 April 2015 cars with actual unrounded CO_2 emissions of 75g/km which are not zero-emission cars (see Tip 27) are charged to tax at only 5% of their list price. This makes very low emission cars a tax-efficient benefit.

Choose A Very Low Emission Car For A 5% Charge

Charlie is environmentally conscious. He needs a company car for work, but chooses a small, low emission model with CO_2 emissions of 70g/km. The car has a list price of £10,000.

The car is a very low emission car for which the appropriate percentage is 5%. Consequently the cash equivalent of the benefit for 2013/14 is only £500.

If Charlie is a basic rate taxpayer, he will pay tax of only £100 on the benefit of the car. If he is a higher rate taxpayer, the tax charge is still only £200 for 2013/14.

24. Choose A Cheaper Car

As the cash equivalent of the benefit of a company car is a percentage of the price of that car (as adjusted for periods of unavailability and private use contributions), it follows that less tax is payable on a cheaper car than on a more expensive model with equivalent CO2 emissions.

Consequently, choosing a cheaper car will reduce the tax paid in respect of the car throughout the period for which it is allocated to the employee.

Choose A Cheaper Car

William has a company car with a list price of £12,000. His colleague James chooses an expensive model with a list price of £50,000. Both cars have CO_2 emissions of 180g/km, which equates to an appropriate percentage of 28% for 2013/14.

William is taxed on a cash equivalent of £3,360 (£12,000 @ 28%) in respect of the benefit of his car. This equates to a tax charge of £1,344 for a higher rate taxpayer.

By contrast, James is taxed on a cash equivalent of £14,000 (£50,000 @ 28%). This equates to a tax charge of £5,600 for a higher rate taxpayer.

By choosing a more expensive car James will pay considerably more tax than William for each year that the cars are available to them.

25. List Price Versus Price Actually Paid

The tax charge on the benefit of a company car is determined by reference to the list price of the car, which may be very different to the price actually paid.

The list price of the car is the price published by the car's manufacturer, importer or distributor (as the case may be) as the inclusive price for a car of that kind sold in the UK, singly in a retail sale in the open market on the day before the date of the car's first registration.

This means that where the employer negotiates a discount, the employee does not benefit from the discount. It is always the list price rather than the actual price paid which is used to determine the cash equivalent value of the benefit.

As the price of the car used to calculate the cash equivalent of the benefit is always the list price when the car is new, regardless of the age of the car and its current value, it is rarely tax efficient to provide a second-hand car or an older car as a company car. The amount charged to tax does not reflect the depreciation on the car.

Employees and employers seeking to minimise the tax charge of a company car by choosing a cheaper car need to make their decision by reference to the list price of the car, rather than the price payable by the employer.

List Price Versus Price Actually Paid

Elliot's employer provides him with a company car. The employer purchased the car when it was two years old for a price of £10,000. The list price of the car when new was £18,000.

The tax charge is computed by reference to the list price of the car on the day before first registration (i.e. £18,000) rather than the price paid by Elliot's employer when the car was two years old (i.e. £10,000).

Although Elliot is provided with a second hand car with a value of £10,000 he pays tax by reference to the much higher list price.

26. Limit Optional Accessories

The list price of optional accessories is added to the list price of the car when working out the price for the purposes of the tax charge on a company car.

The legislation recognises two types of accessories – standard accessories that are provided with the car and which are reflected in the list price of the car and optional (or additional) accessories which are added extras, the price of which must be taken into account.

The lower the price of the car, the less tax is paid on the benefit of the company car. Limiting or prohibiting the addition of optional accessories can help keep the tax bill down.

Limit Optional Accessories

Olga is choosing her new company car. The car has a list price of £15,000. She is debating whether to opt for an accessories pack which has a list price of £2,000. Choosing the accessories will increase the price of the car to £17,000 for the purposes of working out the company car tax charge.

Assuming an appropriate percentage of 25%, choosing the accessory pack will increase the cash equivalent value of the car by £500 and the tax payable by a higher rate taxpayer by £200.

27. Drive An Electric Company Car Tax-Free

It is possible to enjoy a company car tax-free until 5 April 2015 if you choose an electric car or another car which is not capable of emitting CO_2 engine emissions in any circumstances.

Providing a zero-emission car is also beneficial from the employer's perspective as there are no Class 1A National Insurance Contributions to pay.

Drive An Electric Company Car Tax-Free

Holly chooses an electric car as her company car. As the car is a zero-emission car, the appropriate percentage is 0% until 5 April 2015.

Holly is able to enjoy the benefit of her electric company car tax-free.

28. Tax-Free Company Cars For Lower Paid Employees

The benefit of a company car is only taxable when provided to employees earning at the rate of £8,500 a year (P11D employees) or to directors.

No tax charge arises when a company car is provided to an employee earning at a rate of less than £8,500 a year (P9D employee), although the cash equivalent of the benefit is taken into account in determining if the £8,500 threshold is reached.

If after taking account of benefits provided to the employee, the employee is lower paid, a company car can be provided free of tax.

Tax-Free Company Cars For Lower Paid Employees

Lucinda works one day a week. She has a cash salary of £3,000 and a company car with a cash equivalent value of £3,000.

As her earning rate is £6,000 she is lower paid and able to enjoy the benefit of the company car tax-free.

29. Cars For Family Members

The tax charge on a company car arises where a car is made available by reason of employment for the private use of the employee or 'a member of his family or household'.

While it may seem attractive to provide a car to a lower paid family member rather than to a P11D employee to avoid the tax charge, this may be challenged by HMRC unless it can be shown that it is usual to provide a car to other employees with a similar job and level of pay as the lower paid employee.

Cars For Family Members

Jack is a senior manager and entitled to a car as part of his job. His wife Ellen also works for the company in an administrative role one day a week, earning £4,000 a year.

The car has a cash equivalent value of £3,000.

The family only need one car and it is suggested that it would be tax effective to provide it to Ellen rather than to Jack as the car would be a tax-free benefit in her hands as her earnings rate is less than £8,500 (see Tip 28).

However, employees of Ellen's grade are not usually provided with company cars and the provision is likely to be challenged by HMRC with the result that Jack would remain liable for the car benefit tax. Tax planning of this nature is not recommended unless the provision of the lower-paid family member can be justified in its own right.

30. Limit Capital Contributions To £5,000

The price of the car for the purposes of working out the taxable benefit of a company car is the list price of the car plus the list price of any optional accessories, less any capital contributions made by the employee.

An employer may allow an employee to make capital contributions in order to choose a more expensive car. However, for the purposes of the benefit calculation, capital contributions can only reduce the price of the car by up to £5,000. Capital contributions in excess of £5,000 are of no benefit in reducing the tax charge and the excess may be better utilised as a private use contribution.

Capital contributions are rarely worthwhile from a tax perspective, unless the employee keeps the car for number of years and drives a car with a high appropriate percentage (although they may enable the employee to drive the car of their choice). The tax saved will depend on the appropriate percentage and the employee's marginal rate of tax.

Limit Capital Contributions To £5,000

Alfie chooses a company car with a list price of £32,000, making a capital contribution of £7,000.

Although Alfie's employer has only met £25,000 of the costs (£32,000 - £7,000), the price for the purposes of working out the taxable benefit on the company car is £27,000 (£32,000 - £5,000) as the reduction for the capital contribution is capped at £5,000.

Assuming an appropriate percentage of 25%, the cash equivalent of the benefit is £6,750. Had Alfie not made the contribution, the cash equivalent would have been £8,000.

Making the contribution reduces the cash equivalent value by £1,250. Assuming Alfie is a higher rate taxpayer this saves him tax of £500 a year. Assuming he keeps the car for three years (and appropriate percentages and tax rates are unchanged), his capital contribution of £7,000 will only save him tax of £1,500.

The same result would have been obtained for a contribution of £5,000.

31. Private Use Contributions

An employer may require the employee to make a contribution as a condition for the car being available for private use. Whilst this will not eliminate the tax charge it will reduce the cash equivalent on which tax is charged. However, this is only the case if the employee is required to make a payment as a condition of the car being made available for private use and does in fact make the payment.

Any contributions for private use are deducted after the application of the appropriate percentage and any adjustment to reflect periods of unavailability. The cash equivalent is not reduced if the employee makes the payments voluntarily.

The tax saved will be less than the amount of the contributions and consequently private use contributions are not effective from a tax perspective.

Private Use Contributions

Oliver has a company car with a list price of £30,000 and an appropriate percentage of 28%. As a condition of the car being available for his private use, he is required to make a private use contribution of £50 per month. Oliver is a higher rate taxpayer.

The cash equivalent of the benefit before taking account of the capital contribution is £8,400. This is reduced by £600 (12 x £50) to £7,800 to reflect the private use contribution. Oliver must pay tax of £3,120 on the benefit for the tax year in question.

Making the private use contribution has saved Oliver tax of £240. He would have been better off to the tune of £360 (£600 - £240) had he not made the contribution and paid the higher tax charge. Each £1 paid by way of a private use contribution only saves Oliver 40p in tax.

32. Periods Of Unavailability Of Less Than 30 Days

The cash equivalent of the benefit of a company car is proportionately reduced to reflect periods at the start of the tax year before the car is first made available, periods at the end of the tax year after the car has ceased to be available and other periods of at least 30 days when the car is unavailable. The 30-day period can span two tax years.

However, no reduction is given if the car is unavailable for a period of less than 30 days and the employee is taxed as if he or she had the use of the car throughout the period of unavailability. If the car is expensive or has high CO_2 emissions, short periods of unavailability can work out expensive.

Where a period of unavailability is just short of 30 days, it may be beneficial not to return the car to the employee until the 30-day mark has passed to secure the reduction.

See Tip 33 below where a replacement car is provided during a period of unavailability.

Periods Of Unavailability Of Less Than 30 Days

Frank has a company car with a list price of £40,000 and an appropriate percentage of 30%. The car is involved in an accident in June 2013 and off the road for 25 days. As the period of unavailability was less than 30 days there is no reduction in the cash equivalent of the benefit.

However, had the garage retained the car for a further five days the cash equivalent would have been reduced by £986 (30/365 x (£40,000 x 30%)).

Assuming Frank is a higher rate taxpayer, keeping the car off the road for a further five days would save him £394 (£984 x 40%) in tax.

33. Beware Superior Replacements

As illustrated in Tip 32 above, no reduction is made to the cash equivalent value to reflect periods of unavailability of less than 30 days.

Where a company car is off the road for repair, the employee is usually provided with a replacement. To prevent a double charge from arising, the replacement is ignored where the original car is off the road for less than 30 days as long as the replacement car is not materially better than the original.

If a superior replacement is provided, this need not be a problem if it can be shown that this was the only car available. For example, if an employee's Mondeo is off the road and the employee is provided with a BMW by way of replacement and the BMW is the only car available, the employee may escape a separate tax charge on the replacement, despite the fact it is superior to his allocated car.

However, if the employee is deliberately provided with a superior replacement, he or she will be taxed on both the original car for the full year and on the superior replacement for the period that it was available.

Beware The Superior Replacement

Dave has a company car with a list price of £20,000 and an appropriate percentage of 25%.

The car is involved in an accident and is off the road for 20 days.

During this time Dave is given a replacement car. As his daughter's wedding is due to take place while Dave's car is off the road, the boss provides him with a Mercedes with a list price of £50,000 and an appropriate percentage of 28%.

Other cars were available as replacements.

As Dave has deliberately been provided with a superior model, he suffers the tax charge for the full year on his main car (which has a cash equivalent value of £5,000), because no reduction is given for the period that it was off the road as this was less than 30 days.

He is also taxed on the replacement car because this is materially better than the original.

34. Cash Alternative To A Company Car

Rather than suffer the tax burden on a company car, an employee may prefer to receive a cash alternative and instead buy or lease a car privately. Many employers now offer employees the choice between a company car and a cash alternative.

Where an employee is offered the choice between a company car and a cash alternative, the employee is taxed by reference to whichever he or she chooses. If the employee chooses the company car, the benefit is taxed in accordance with the company car tax rules. If the employee chooses the cash alternative, this is taxed as extra salary and is subject to PAYE and NIC in the usual way. However, in working out the employee's earnings rate in order to ascertain whether the employee is lower paid or not, where a cash alternative is offered the earnings rate is determined using whichever is of higher value – the cash alternative or the cash equivalent of the company car.

Where an employee takes a cash alternative and uses a private car for business travel, the company car rules do not apply. Mileage allowances paid for business travel will instead be subject to the AMAP rules (see Tip 7).

Whether the employee is better off taking a cash alternative and privately funding a car or opting for a company car will depend on a range of factors. Each case must be evaluated individually.

35. Planning Ahead For Future Tax Changes

The company car tax rules are constantly being tweaked and the emissions criteria are tightened each year, meaning that an employee who does not change his or her car will pay more tax (assuming tax rates are unchanged) for the privilege of having a company car in future tax years than in the current one, regardless of the fact that the car being driven is older and will have depreciated in value.

The zero charge for electric and other zero-emission cars comes to an end on 5 April 2015 and two new lower bands are introduced from that date. Therefore the window for having a tax-free electric car (see Tip 27) is limited. Employees with electric company cars will need to decide whether to remain within the company car regime once their car ceases to be a tax-free benefit.

At present the cash equivalent is capped at 35% of the list price. The maximum charge is increased to 37% from 2015/16. Tighter emissions criteria will mean more drivers will suffer the maximum charge. Drivers of high emission cars may wish to consider swapping to a more environmentally friendly model before 6 April 2015 to prevent a hike in the tax payable on their car.

Currently, diesel cars are charged at an additional 3% compared to a petrol model with the same CO_2 emissions (subject to the maximum charge). The diesel supplement is being removed from 6 April 2016, meaning that from that date diesel cars will have the same appropriate percentage as a petrol car with the same level of emissions. This means that diesel cars will be a lower tax option in the future.

It is important that employers and employees keep abreast of changes in the rules and take protective action where necessary to mitigate the impact of any tax rises.

Planning Ahead For Future Company Car Changes

Helga drives a company car with CO_2 emissions of 210g/km. The price of the car for company car tax purposes is £30,000. Helga is a higher rate taxpayer. It is assumed that the higher rate of income tax remains at 40%.

In 2013/14 the cash equivalent of the benefit is £10,200 (£30,000 @ 34%). Helga pays tax on the benefit of £4,080.

In 2014/15 the cash equivalent of the benefit will be £10,500 (£30,000 @ 35%). Helga will pay tax on the benefit of £4,200.

In 2015/16 the cash equivalent of benefit will be £11,100 (£30,000 @ 37%). Helga will pay tax on the benefit of £4,440.

If Helga keeps the same car, she will pay £360 more in tax in 2015/16 than in 2013/14 as a result of more stringent emissions criteria and an increase in the maximum charge.

Helga has the option to change her car on 6 April 2014. Mindful of the increasing tax burden she switches to a car with emissions of 180g/km and a price of £25,000. The car has an appropriate percentage of 29% in 2014/15. This will reduce her tax bill to £2,900 in 2014/15. The cash equivalent of the benefit is £7,250 (£25,000 @ 29%) and the tax thereon at 40% is £2,900. Swapping her car saves her £1,300 in tax in 2014/15 alone.

36. Free Fuel – A Worthwhile Benefit?

Petrol is expensive and having your petrol costs paid by your employer may seem like an attractive benefit. However, the tax costs of free fuel have increased significantly in recent years and unless your private mileage is very high it is unlikely to be a worthwhile benefit.

The cash equivalent of the benefit of employer-provided fuel is found by multiplying the appropriate percentage, as found for the purposes of computing the company car tax benefit by the set figure for the tax year in question. Thus, the higher the car's CO_2 emissions, the higher the amount charged to tax in respect of free fuel.

For 2013/14 the car fuel multiplier is set at £21,100.

Free Fuel – A Worthwhile Benefit?

Emma has a company car with CO_2 emissions of 160g/m. The car is a petrol car and the appropriate percentage for 2013/14 is 24%.

Emma receives free fuel for private motoring in her company car. For 2013/14 the cash equivalent of the benefit is £5,064. As a higher rate taxpayer, the benefit of free fuel costs Emma £2,025.60 in tax.

Emma drives 10,000 private miles a year and fuel consumption is 8.8 miles a litre. She therefore uses 1,136 litres of fuel for private purposes a year. At £1.40 per litre, fuel for private motoring will cost her £1,590. This is £435.60 less than she pays in tax on the benefit of free fuel.

Therefore Emma would be better off giving up the free fuel and paying for private fuel herself. Taking a cash alternative to the fuel benefit if offered would leave her much better off.

37. Impact Of Car Choice On Fuel Benefit

The same appropriate percentage is used to calculate both the company car tax benefit and the car fuel benefit. The appropriate percentage depends on the level of CO_2 emissions of the car. Consequently, the choice of car, and more importantly whether the car has high or low emissions, affects both the tax payable on the car and also on fuel where this is provided.

Choosing a high emission car will mean a double whammy from a tax perspective, whereas a low emission car will generate double the savings.

Impact Of Car Choice On Fuel Benefit

Susan chooses a small low emission petrol car with CO_2 emissions of 120g/km. The appropriate percentage for 2013/14 is 16%. She also receives free fuel from her employer.

The cash equivalent of Susan's fuel benefit is £3,376 for 2013/14. Assuming Susan is a higher rate taxpayer, she will pay £1,350 in tax for the benefit of free fuel.

Sophie also has a company car. She has chosen a petrol model with CO_2 emissions of 230g/km. For 2013/14 she is subject to the maximum appropriate percentage of 35%.

The cash equivalent of Sophie's fuel benefit is £7,385 in 2013/14. As she is a higher rate taxpayer, she will pay £2,954 in tax for the benefit of free fuel – £1,604 more than that paid by Susan.

Choosing a low emission car reduces the tax payable in respect of both the car and employer-provided fuel.

38. Free Fuel – A More Expensive Benefit Than A Company Car?

The multiplier used for the purposes of working out the cash equivalent of the fuel benefit has increased significantly in recent years. In 2007/08 the multiplier was £14,400. By 2013/14, it had increased to £21,100 (a rise of 46%). The multiplier is set to rise in line with inflation each year.

The current level of £21,100 is more than the cost of many cars. Thus, even if an employee seeks to minimise the tax payable on their company car by choosing a cheaper, low emission model, they could easily end up paying more in tax for the benefit of free fuel than for the benefit of the car. This will be the case wherever the price of the car for company car tax purposes is less than the fuel multiplier.

In this scenario the employee may wish to re-evaluate whether free fuel remains a worthwhile benefit.

Free Fuel – A More Expensive Benefit Than A Company Car?

Roger has a company car. He is keen to minimise the tax cost of the car and chooses a relatively cheap model costing £15,000 with CO_2 emissions of 115g/km.

The car is a petrol car and for 2013/14 the appropriate percentage is 15%.

Roger also receives fuel for private motoring in his company car.

For 2013/14 the cash equivalent of the car benefit is £2,250 (£15,000 @ 15%). As a higher rate taxpayer, Roger pays tax of £900 on the benefit.

The cash equivalent of the fuel benefit for 2013/14 is £3,165 (£21,100 @ 15%). As a higher rate taxpayer, Roger pays tax of £1,266 on the benefit of free fuel.

As the fuel multiplier is higher than the price of the car, Roger pays more in tax for the benefit of the fuel (by £366) than for the benefit of the car.

39. Making Good The Cost Of Private Fuel

Where the employer provides fuel for motoring in the company car, the fuel benefit charge can be avoided if the employee is required to make good the cost of fuel used for private purposes and actually does so.

It is important that both these conditions are met if the charge is to be avoided.

The advisory fuel rates published by HMRC (see Tip 11) can be used to set the rate at which the employee is required to make good the cost of private fuel.

Making Good The Cost Of Private Fuel

Graeme has a company car and undertakes a high level of business mileage. His employer has provided him with a fuel card to pay for his petrol. However, as a condition of the availability of the car, Graeme is required to make good the cost of private fuel. The reimbursement is made by deduction from his salary at the current advisory rate as set by HMRC.

As Graeme is both required to make good the cost of fuel for private motoring and actually does so, he does not suffer a fuel benefit charge.

40. Avoid Partial Reimbursement

The fuel benefit charge does not apply if the employee is required to make good the cost of fuel provided for private motoring and actually does so (see Tip 39). However, the fuel benefit charge is an all or nothing charge and there is no proportionate reduction if the employee makes good some of the cost of private motoring but not all of it. The fuel benefit charge will apply in full, even if the employee has made good some of the cost.

This should be avoided in all circumstances.

Avoid Partial Reimbursement

Nathan has a company car. He pays for fuel on a fuel card provided by his employer. He is required to make a contribution of £50 per month towards the cost of private fuel, which is deducted from his salary each month.

During the tax year in question, the cost of fuel used by Nathan for private motoring is £1,600.

As he has not made good the total cost of free fuel, Nathan is liable to the fuel benefit in full. Paying £50 per month towards the cost is ineffective from a tax perspective.

41. Making Good – Beware The Timing Trap

As noted in Tip 39, the fuel benefit charge can be avoided if the employee is required to make good the cost of fuel used for private motoring and actually does so.

The legislation requires the making good to be done 'in the tax year in question'. However, in practice it is likely that there will be a delay in making good, for example because mileage records for the final tax month of the year are not available until after the end of the tax year or because the sums in respect of private mileage are deducted from the employee's salary one month in arrears.

Where the sum has not been made good in full before the end of the tax year, HMRC will accept that the condition has been fulfilled as long as there is no unreasonable delay in making good. However, HMRC's discretion should not be relied on and steps should be taken to ensure the employee makes good the cost of free fuel in a timely manner. Unreasonable delays may mean that the employee is faced with a tax charge for the fuel benefit in full.

42. Withdrawing Provision Of Free Fuel

If the provision of employer-provided fuel for private motoring in a company car is withdrawn part way through the tax year, the fuel scale benefit is proportionately reduced (as long as the provision of fuel is not reinstated before the end of the tax year – see Tip 43).

The extent to which free fuel is beneficial should be kept under review and consideration should be given to withdrawing the benefit if the employee's private mileage drops to a level where it is no longer a worthwhile benefit as this will reduce the tax payable.

Withdrawing Provision Of Free Fuel

Stephen's employer relocates from Nottingham to Milton Keynes in March 2013. Stephen initially commutes from his home just outside Nottingham to his new office in Milton Keynes. He has a company car and his employer also provides fuel for private motoring.

On 1 September 2013 he moves house. His new home is only six miles from his new office. As a result of the move, his private mileage falls significantly, such that it is cheaper for Stephen to meet the cost of private mileage than to pay the tax on the fuel benefit.

The benefit of employer-provided fuel is withdrawn from 6 September 2013.

Stephen drives a petrol car with an appropriate percentage of 22% for 2013/14.

The cash equivalent of the fuel benefit would be £4,642 (£21,100 @ 22%) were fuel provided for the full 2013/14 tax year. Assuming Stephen is a higher rate taxpayer, this would cost him £1,856 in tax.

As the provision of free fuel is withdrawn from 6 September 2013, Stephen only has the benefit of free fuel for five months of the 2013/14 tax year. Consequently the cash equivalent of the fuel benefit is reduced to £1,934 (5/12 x £4,642) to reflect this, reducing Steve's tax bill to £774.

43. Beware Of Reinstating Free Fuel

As noted in Tip 42, the fuel benefit is proportionately reduced where the benefit of free fuel is withdrawn part way through the tax year. However, if the provision of free fuel is reinstated before the end of the tax year, the reduction is lost and the fuel benefit charge is applied for the full year without reduction.

Where the employee and employer wish to reinstate the provision of free fuel previously withdrawn it may be better to wait until the start of the next tax year. Consideration could be given to the provision of a cash alternative in the interim.

Beware Of Reinstating Free Fuel

Ryan has a company car and has been provided with fuel for private motoring for a number of years. As a result of the rise in the multiplier for 2013/14, he decides the benefit is no longer worthwhile and agrees with his employer for the provision of free fuel to be withdrawn from 6 May 2013.

In February 2014 his elderly mother moves into a residential home some distance away and he visits her every weekend. As a result his private mileage increases and he considers that it would worthwhile receiving free fuel for private motoring. To avoid a high fuel charge for 2013/14, the reinstatement is delayed until 6 April 2014.

Ryan drives a petrol car with an appropriate percentage of 25% in 2013/14.

If the provision of free fuel is reinstated before 6 April 2014, Ryan will suffer the fuel benefit charge for the full 2013/14 tax year. The cash equivalent of the benefit would be £5,275 (£21,100 @ 25%), which assuming Ryan is a higher rate taxpayer would cost him £2,110 in tax.

However, if the reinstatement is delayed until 6 April 2014, Ryan only suffers the fuel benefit charge for one month in 2013/14. The cash equivalent of the benefit is therefore £440 (£5,275 x 1/12) and the tax thereon £176. Delaying the reinstatement of free fuel saves Ryan £1,934 in tax and ensures he receives the benefit for the months for which he did not receive free fuel.

44. Pool Cars

Some employers may find it preferable to have a pool of cars available for use by employees whenever they need a car for a business journey, rather than allocating specific cars to individual employees.

This can be beneficial from a tax and National Insurance perspective as no tax charge arises on the employee in relation to the use of a pool car, and consequently there is no Class 1A liability on the employer.

However, it important that the conditions applying in relation to pool cars are met to avoid triggering a taxable benefit in relation to the car. The conditions are as follows:

- the car is made available to and used by more than one employee by reason of his or her employment;
- the car is not ordinarily used by one employee to the exclusion of others;
- any private use by any employee is 'merely incidental' to the business use of the car; and
- the car is not normally kept overnight near the home of the employee.

Given the tax at stake it is unsurprising that HMRC apply the rules strictly and take a harsh line. It is not enough to simply label a car a 'pool car'. If the car is available for the employee's private use, a car benefit charge will apply.

45. Unrestricted Private Use Of A Company Van

Unless private use of a company van is restricted or insignificant, a tax charge will arise where a company van is available for the private use of an employee.

Unlike the charge on company cars, the van benefit charge does not depend on the price of the van or its CO_2 emissions. Instead, all vans are equal from a tax perspective and the cash equivalent of the van benefit is set at £3,000 for 2013/14. This equates to a tax bill of £600 for a basic rate taxpayer, £1,200 for a higher rate taxpayer and £1,350 for an additional rate taxpayer.

The charge is proportionately reduced if the van is unavailable, either at the start of the tax year before being allocated to the employee, at the end of the tax year after ceasing to be available or for a period of 30 days or more. No reduction is given for periods of unavailability of less than 30 days.

The van benefit charge only arises where the van is provided to a P11D employee or director. No charge arises where a van is available for the private use of a P9D employee, although the cash equivalent of the van benefit is taken into account in determining the employee's earnings rate.

Unrestricted Private Use Of A Company Van

Jason is allocated a company van by his employer. The van is available for his private use without restriction.

Jason is taxed on the benefit arising from the availability of the van for his private use. For 2013/14 the cash equivalent of the benefit is £3,000. Jason is a basic rate taxpayer and pays tax of £600 for the private use of the van.

46. Tax-Free Home To Work Travel In A Company Van

By restricting the private use of a company van it is possible for an employee to use a company van for home to work travel without triggering the van benefit charge.

A tax charge can be avoided if the terms on which the van is made available to the employee prohibit private use of the van other than for ordinary commuting and the van is used mainly for the purposes of the employee's business travel. Ordinary commuting is the employee's normal home to work journey.

It should be noted that any insignificant private use is disregarded in determining whether the commuter requirement is met. Insignificant private use would include making a slight detour on the way home to collect a child from school or occasionally using the van to take a large item to the tip. However, more significant private use, such as regularly using the van for shopping trips, would trigger the tax charge.

Tax-Free Home To Work Travel In A Company Van

Ralph is employed as a blind fitter and allocated a van by his employer. The van is used mainly for Ralph's business travel, but Ralph is allowed to keep the van at home and use it for his journey to work. All other private use is prohibited.

Ralph meets the restricted private use condition and as such the van benefit charge does not apply. He is able to use the van for home to work travel without triggering a tax charge.

47. Shared Vans – Family Member Trap

A van may be made available to more than one employee who shares the van and to whom it is available for private use.

Where a van is shared, the cash equivalent of the benefit is calculated in the usual way, taking account of periods of unavailability. The cash equivalent is apportioned between all sharers, including any P9D employees who are not taxed on their share of the benefit.

However, the rules are modified where two members of the same family or household share a van and one member of the family is a P9D employee. In this case, the P9D employee is ignored and the full charge is levied on the other employee.

Shared Vans – Family Member Trap

Alex, Sam and Toby work for the same employer and share a van. The van Is available for their private use. Alex is a P9D employee and Sam and Toby are P11D employees.

The van is available throughout 2013/14 and the men have equal use of it. The cash equivalent of the benefit of £3,000 is shared equally. Toby and Sam each suffer a tax charge based on their share of the benefit (£1,000 each). As Alex is a P9D employee he is not taxed on his share.

Chris and his son Will live in the family home. They work for the same employer and also share a van, which is available to both of them for their private use.

Chris is a P9D employee and Will is a P11D employee. As they are members of the same family and household, the anti-avoidance rules come into play.

Chris's use of the van is ignored for the purposes of allocating the benefit and Will is taxed on the full equivalent value of £3,000 despite not having exclusive use of the van.

48. Private Fuel For Vans

As with company cars a separate charge arises where fuel is made available for private use in a company van. However, there are differences which mean providing fuel for private motoring in a company van can be a worthwhile benefit.

The van scale charge applies where fuel is provided for unrestricted private motoring in a company van. It is set at a fixed level, which for 2013/14 is £564.

As with company car fuel, the charge is reduced to reflect periods for which the van was unavailable. The charge can also be eliminated if the employee is required to make good the cost of fuel for private journeys and actually does so. There is no charge if fuel is only provided for business journeys.

As noted in Tip 46, there is no tax charge in respect of the provision of the van if the private use of the van is restricted for home to work travel. This is mirrored in the fuel charge so that no fuel benefit arises where this condition is met. This means that the employer can meet the cost of fuel for the employee's home to work travel in the van tax-free. This is a worthwhile perk.

Private Fuel For Vans

Greg is provided with a van by his employer, which is used mainly for business journeys. He is also able to use the van for home to work travel, although other private use of the van is prohibited.

His employer pays for all fuel for the van.

As the restricted private use condition is met there is no tax charge on the benefit of the van or the provision of the use. Consequently, Greg is able to enjoy the benefit of free home to work travel tax-free.

49. Tax-Free Cars For Disabled Employees

Provided that certain conditions are met, it is possible to provide a car for the use of a disabled employee for home to work travel without the employee incurring a tax charge in respect of the car.

However, this only applies if each of the following three conditions is met:

- the car has been adapted for the disabled employee's special needs or the car is an automatic car and because of the employee's disability he or she is only able to drive an automatic car;
- the terms on which the car is made available prohibit use other than for business travel or for home to work commuting; and
- in the tax year in question, the car is only used in accordance with these terms.

It should be noted that if the terms are breached, for example if the car is used for private purposes other than home to work travel, the exemption does not apply and the car benefit charge applies in the usual way.

Tax-Free Cars For Disabled Employees

Karen is registered as disabled. Because of her disabilities, she finds it difficult to use public transport. Her employer provides her with a car which has been adapted to her needs. The car is available for business use and home to work travel. Other private use is prohibited.

As the conditions for exemption are met, Karen can use the car for home to work travel tax free.

50. Automatic Cars For Disabled Employees

Automatic cars are generally more expensive than their manual equivalent.

Where a disabled employee is provided with a company car and because of his or her disability the employee can only drive a car with automatic transmission, the price of the equivalent manual model is used for the purposes of working out the car benefit charge.

This adjustment should not be overlooked as will save tax each year for which the car is made available to the employee.

Automatic Cars For Disabled Employees

Edward is registered as disabled and as a result of his disabilities can only drive a car with automatic transmission. He is provided with a company car by his employer, which is available for his private use.

He is allocated an automatic car, the list price of which is £1,000 more than the equivalent manual model. The car has an appropriate percentage of 28% for 2013/14. Edward is a higher rate taxpayer.

By using the price of the equivalent manual model, Edward saves tax of £112 in 2013/14 ((£1,000 @ 28%) x 40%).

Chapter 4.
Family And Welfare Benefits

51. Workplace Nurseries

Childcare is expensive and any help given in this area to working parents is generally highly valued and can help in retaining staff.

Larger employees with reasonable numbers of employees who have young children may wish to consider setting up a workplace nursery.

This can be an extremely valuable benefit as far as the employee is concerned. Provided the associated conditions are met, there is no tax charge on the benefit. Unlike the exemption for employer supported childcare and childcare vouchers there is no limit on the value of the care that can be provided tax free.

To qualify for the exemption, the childcare facility must have the appropriate registrations and approvals, childcare must be available to all employees who require it and the children for whom the care is provided must be employees' children or children for whom the employees have parental responsibility. The nursery does not have to be based at the employer's premises. It can be elsewhere as long as the care is not provided in residential premises and the employer is involved in the management and finance of the facility.

Several employers can join forces to provide a workplace nursery for the use of their collective employees. This can help spread the cost and make setting up a workplace nursery a more viable option.

Workplace Nurseries

Gabby works on an industrial estate. She has two small children aged one and three. The employers on the estate have joined together to provide a workplace nursery on the estate for use by employees' children.

Gabby works three days a week and uses the nursery to provide childcare for her children while she is working.

The conditions for exemption are met and Gabby is not taxed on the benefit of the childcare she receives. This is a valuable benefit as if the nursery were not available it would cost her £360 a week in childcare.

52. Employer-Supported Childcare

Running a workplace nursery (see Tip 51) may not be a viable option for all employers. However, there are still ways in which employers can provide help with employees' childcare costs in a tax-efficient manner.

Where an employer provides help by contracting directly with a commercial childcare provider, as long as the associated conditions are met, the resulting benefit is tax free up to the employee's exempt amount.

The exempt amount depends on when the employee joined the employer's childcare scheme. The exempt amount is £55 per week if the employee joined the employer's childcare scheme before 6 April 2011, regardless of the employee's marginal rate of tax. However, where the employee joined the scheme on or after 6 April 2011, the relief is worth £11 per week to all employees and the exempt amount depends on the employee's marginal rate of tax.

For 2013/14 the exempt amount is £55 per week for a basic rate taxpayer, £28 per week for a higher rate taxpayer and £25 per week for an additional rate taxpayer.

Where the value of care provided exceeds the employee's exempt amount, the excess is taxable.

An employee is only allowed one exempt amount to cover both employer-supported childcare and childcare vouchers and regardless of the number of children for whom care is provided.

Employer-Supported Childcare

Joanna has two children aged two and four. She works four days a week. Her children are looked after by a registered childminder. Her employer meets the cost of her childcare and contracts directly with childminder. The care costs £200 per week.

Joanna joined the employer-supported childcare scheme in 2010. She is a higher rate taxpayer. Her exempt amount is £55 per week because she joined the scheme before 6 April 2011.

Joanna receives tax-free childcare of £55 per week. The excess of £145 is subject to tax and is reported to HMRC on her P11D.

53. Childcare Vouchers

As an alternative to contracting with a childminder or commercial nursery, an employer may choose to provide childcare support in the form of vouchers.

Childcare vouchers are exempt up to the employee's exempt amount (for which see Tip 52), as long as the exempt amount has not already been used against employer provided care.

Childcare vouchers are often provided by means of salary sacrifice arrangements (for which see Tip 2).

Example – Childcare Vouchers

Jean returns to work in September 2013 when her daughter Chloe is ten months old. Her employer provides her with nursery vouchers of £50 per week to help with her childcare costs. Jean is a higher rate taxpayer.

As Jean joined her employer's childcare scheme after 5 April 2011 and is a higher rate taxpayer, her exempt amount for 2013/14 is £28 per week. This means that she can receive £28 of childcare vouchers tax-free each week. The balance of £22 per week is taxable.

54. Beware Reimbursing Employees' Childcare Costs

The exemption for employer-supported childcare (see Tip 52) only applies where the employer contracts directly with the childminder or the commercial nursery for the provision of care. It does not apply where the contract is between the employee and the childcare provider and the employer either pays the bill on the employee's behalf or reimburses the employee's childcare costs. In these cases the benefit of the tax-free amount is lost.

Where the employer pays the bill on the employee's behalf this is known as settling a pecuniary liability and the amount paid should be returned on the employee's P11D.

While the employee pays the childcare costs initially and reclaims these from the employer, the amount reimbursed is taxed as earnings and is liable to PAYE tax and Class 1 National Insurance as for payments of wages and salary.

This is an easy trap for the unwary to fall into.

Beware Reimbursing Employees' Childcare Costs

Rose is aware of exemptions for childcare costs and her employer agrees to meet the costs of her childminder up to her exempt amount. Rose is a basic rate taxpayer and has an exempt amount of £55 per week for 2013/14.

Rose pays her childminder initially and claims back £55.

However, Rose and her employer have fallen foul of the rules as the employer must contract directly with the childminder. Rose does not benefit from the exempt amount and the £55 reimbursed is taxable as earnings and liable to Class 1 National Insurance.

55. Private Medical Insurance

Private medical insurance is a popular benefit and one that many employers provide for their employees.

However, unlike other benefits there is no tax exemption and where private medical insurance is provided for P11D employees or directors, the employee or director is taxed on the provision of the benefit.

The amount charged to tax is the cost of providing the benefit less any amount made good by the employee. Class 1A National Insurance is payable by the employer.

There is no tax charge where private medical insurance is provided for P9D employees.

Despite the lack of tax exemption, employer-provided medical insurance can be beneficial. Employers are likely to be able to negotiate discounts on group policies and it will always be cheaper to pay the tax on the benefit than to meet the full cost of the insurance from net pay.

Private Medical Insurance

Robert looks into the cost of private medical insurance and finds that it would cost him £60 per month. His employer offers employees the option of private medical insurance. This is a taxable benefit. Due to group discounts, it costs Robert's employer £50 per month for equivalent cover.

Robert is a higher rate taxpayer.

If Robert takes the benefit, he is taxed on the cost to the employer (£600). This will cost him £240 a year in tax.

If Robert provides the cover himself it will cost him £720 a year payable out of his net pay.

Robert is much better off having the benefit despite the tax charge.

56. Eye Tests

Under health and safety legislation employers may be required to provide eye tests for employees who are required to use a computer screen or other VDU.

No taxable benefit arises where the employer provides eye tests for employees that are required under health and safety legislation and the employer does not need to report the provision of the eye tests to HMRC.

Where the eye test shows that the employee needs glasses or other optical aids for VDU work, the employer can provide these without triggering a tax charge. However, the glasses must be required for VDU work only, rather than for general use. Where the conditions are met, there is no limit on the costs of glasses or lenses that can be provided for VDU work tax free. Provided the employer is willing to meet the bill, the employee can choose a designer pair tax free.

Eye Tests

Bethany is required to look at a computer screen as part of her work. Her employer is obliged to provide eye tests under the health and safety legislation. The eye test shows Bethany needs glasses for VDU work. The cost of the glasses is met by the employer. Bethany only uses the glasses for work.

As the terms of the exemption are met, Bethany does not suffer a tax charge on the provision of the eye test or of the glasses.

57. Health Screening And Medical Check-Ups

It is beneficial for employers to have a fit and healthy workforce, as sickness absence is costly for the employer. Many employers offer employees health screening assessments and medical check-ups in a bid to help their workforce stay healthy and to identify health problems early.

Where these are offered, employees can benefit from one health screening assessment and one medical check-up each year free of tax. Any additional health screenings or check-ups will give rise to a taxable benefit. The amount charged to tax is the cost to the employer less any amount made good by the employee.

For these purposes a health screening assessment is an assessment to identify employees who may be at particular risk of ill health and a medical check-up is a physical examination for the sole purpose of determining the employee's state of health. Any treatment provided by the employer is not covered by the exemption and represents a taxable benefit.

Health Screenings And Medical Check-Ups

Josh's employer provides all employees with an annual medical check-up. As a result of the check-up Josh is found to need treatment for a knee injury, the cost of which is met by his employer. The treatment costs £500.

There is no tax charge in respect of the provision of the check-up. However, the cost of the treatment represents a taxable benefit on which Josh must pay tax.

58. Pay A Bonus To Increase SMP

The amount of statutory maternity pay (SMP) that is payable to an employee who is on maternity leave depends on the employee's average weekly earnings.

Employees are paid 90% of average weekly earnings for the first six weeks. The remainder is paid at the standard rate (which is £136.78 for 2013/14) or if less at a rate of 90% of earnings.

Average weekly earnings are calculated by reference to earnings in the relevant period. This is broadly the period ending with the last pay day to fall in or before the qualifying week (which is the 15th week before the week in which the baby is due) and the last normal pay day falling at least eight weeks previously.

Paying a bonus in the relevant period increases the employee's average weekly earnings and the amount of SMP for the first six weeks (and thereafter if 90% of earnings is less than £136.78 per week).

Pay A Bonus To Increase SMP

Poppy is paid £400 per week throughout the relevant period. Her average weekly earnings are £400 per week. At 2013/14 rates she would receive SMP of £360 per week for the first six weeks and £136.78 thereafter.

Poppy is due to be paid a bonus of £3,200 shortly after the end of her relevant period. Her employer advances payment of the bonus so that it falls in her relevant period. This increases her earnings in the eight-week relevant period to £6,400 and her average weekly earnings to £800 per week. This increases the SMP she is due in the first six weeks from £360 per week to £720 per week.

59. Salary Sacrifice – Beware the Statutory Payments Trap

Payment of statutory payments (statutory maternity pay, statutory sick pay, statutory adoption pay, ordinary statutory paternity pay and additional statutory paternity pay) is dependent on an employee meeting various conditions and having average weekly earnings at least equal to the lower earnings limit for Class 1 National Insurance purposes, which for 2013/14 is £109 per week.

Care must be taken where an employee's earnings are not much above this level that entering into a salary sacrifice arrangement does not reduce average weekly earnings below this level and jeopardise entitlement to statutory payments.

60. Welfare Counselling

Although in general the provision of counselling services by an employer to an employee constitutes a taxable benefit, the availability of an exemption makes it possible for employers to provide welfare counselling free of tax. Welfare counselling is counselling other than medical treatment of any kind, advice on finance (other than on debt problems), tax advice, advice on leisure or recreation, or legal advice (other than that provided to employees taking up employee shareholder status).

The exemption is intended to cover counselling in respect of:

- stress
- problems at work
- debt problems
- alcohol and other drug dependency
- career concerns
- bereavement
- equal opportunities
- ill-health
- sexual abuse
- harassment and bullying
- conduct and discipline
- personal relationship difficulties

Welfare Counselling

Katie was finding it difficult to cope following the sudden death of her mother. Her employer arranges for her to receive bereavement counselling and meets the cost. The provision of the counselling does not constitute a taxable benefit.

61. Pension Provision

With the roll-out of auto-enrolment, employers will be required to make pension contributions on behalf of employees. Many employers already contribute to an occupational or personal pension and generous pension provision is an attractive benefit valued by employees.

No tax liability arises in respect of employer contributions to a registered pension scheme. However, the contributions count towards the employee's annual allowance (set at £50,000 for 2013/14 falling to £40,000 from 2014/15). If contributions made by the employer result in the annual allowance being exceeded the employee will suffer the annual allowance tax charge on the excess contributions.

Contributions made by the employer are deductible in computing the employer's taxable profits.

Pension Provision

Henry's employer contributes an amount equal to 5% of his salary to a registered pension scheme. Henry has an annual salary of £40,000. The pension contributions made by his employer of £2,000 per year on his behalf are a tax-free benefit.

Chapter 5.
Other Popular Benefits

62. Mobile Telephones
63. Christmas Parties
64. Sporting And Recreational Facilities
65. Relocation Assistance
66. Suggestion Scheme Awards
67. Long-Service Awards
68. Work-Related Training
69. Additional Costs Of Working From Home
70. Homeworkers – Provision Of Supplies And Equipment
71. Season Ticket Loans

62. Mobile Telephones

The tax exemption for employer-provided mobile phones is well-known and often misunderstood.

Under the terms of the exemption an employer can provide an employee with one mobile phone (or SIM card). The phone can be used for both business and personal calls and the exemption extends to smartphones such as the iPhone and Blackberries. However, devices that have telephone capability but are not used primarily for the purpose of making and receiving calls are outside the scope of the exemption (such as iPads and laptops which use the internet to make calls).

For the exemption to apply, some important conditions must be met:

1. The phone must be made available for the employee's use but ownership of the phone must not be transferred to the employee.
2. The contract must be between the mobile phone company and the employer.

The exemption does not apply if the contract is between the employee and the mobile phone company and the employer either pays the bill on the employee's behalf or reimburses the employee. This sometimes causes problems in practice.

As long as the pitfalls are avoided, employees can enjoy the benefit of a mobile phone tax-free.

Mobile Telephones

XYZ Ltd provides all of its employees with a mobile telephone for their use and meets the costs of all calls whether business or private.

The contract is between XYZ Ltd and the phone company.

Ownership of the phones remains with the employer and the employees must return the phones if they leave.

Each employee is allowed only one employer-provided phone.

The terms of the exemption are met and the employees enjoy the benefit of the mobile phone tax free.

63. Christmas Parties

The exemption for Christmas parties and other annual functions enables employees to enjoy social functions provided at the employer's expense without suffering a tax bill alongside the hangover.

The exemption applies in respect of an annual event (such as a Christmas party or summer ball) which is open to all employees and in respect of which the cost per head is not more than £150. If any of these conditions are not met, the exemption does not apply.

Some points are worthy of note. The £150 per head figure is calculated by reference to all guests, not just employees. If this figure is exceeded, the employee is taxed on the full amount, not just the excess over £150. Where an employee has brought a guest any taxable amount also includes that attributable to the employee's guest. However, no tax charge applies to P9D employees.

The exemption is not limited to one event a year. It can be used for more than one event as long as each meets the qualifying conditions. Where there are several qualifying events but the total cost is more than £150 per head, the exemption can be used so as to give the best result.

Christmas Parties

JKL Ltd holds three events a year – a Christmas party, a summer ball and a Halloween disco. The Christmas party costs £40 per head, the summer ball costs £100 per head and the Halloween disco costs £20 per head.

Although each event qualifies individually, the total of all three events comes to £160, which is more than the £150 allowed by the exemption.

The exemption is best used by applying it to the summer ball (£100 per head) and the Christmas party (£40 per head). As it is an exemption not an allowance the £10 remaining available cannot be set against the Halloween disco, which is a taxable benefit.

To save the employees from suffering a tax charge in respect of the disco, the employer meets the liability arising by means of a PAYE Settlement Agreement.

64. Sporting And Recreational Facilities

It is possible for employers to provide sporting and recreational facilities for employees without triggering a taxable benefit, although the exemption only applies if the facilities are generally available for use by all the employer's employees, the facilities are not available to the general public and the facilities are used mainly by employees or former employees.

The exemption does not apply to facilities provided in residential accommodation, to the provision of holiday or other overnight accommodation or any associated sporting facilities, or to the use of mechanically propelled vehicles, including road vehicles, aircraft and boats.

The exemption enables employers to provide sporting facilities by means of an in-house gym or social club. The facilities can be provided jointly by more than one employer, as long as they are not open to the public. However, a tax liability will arise if the employer provides gym membership or similar for employees at a commercially-run gym or reimburses the cost of an employee's gym membership. This applies regardless of whether the employee takes out a corporate membership at the gym.

Sporting And Recreational Facilities

Alan works for a large employer and is able to use the in-house gym free of charge.

The gym is only available for use by employees.

The exemption applies and no tax liability arises in respect of the provision of this benefit.

Alan's wife Louisa works for a small company. The company has a corporate membership at a commercial gym, which employees are able to use free of charge. The gym is open to members of the public. The exemption does not apply in this case and Louisa will suffer a tax charge in respect of this benefit.

65. Relocation Assistance

Moving house is costly and to encourage employees to take up a new position or to relocate should the company move, many employers offer relocation assistance.

To the extent that certain conditions are met, the first £8,000 of qualifying relocation expenses and benefits can be provided tax-free.

To qualify, the relocation must take place because the employee is starting a new job with the employer, as a result of a change in the employment duties or because of a change in the place where the employment duties are carried out.

Further, the expenses and benefits must relate to one or more of the following:

1. the sale of the employee's old residence;
2. the purchase of the employee's new residence;
3. transporting the employee's belongings to the new residence;
4. any associated travel and subsistence costs;
5. the provision of domestic goods for the new premises;
6. bridging loans.

The expenses and benefits must be provided before the end of the tax year following that in which the change in the employee's job occurred and the new home must be in reasonable daily travelling distance of the new job location where the old home was not.

Qualifying relocation expenses and benefits in excess of £8,000 are taxable as are all non-qualifying expenses and benefits.

Relocation Assistance

Toby takes on a new role within the company and is required to move from the Leicester office to the Manchester office.

He sells his house near Leicester and buys a new home in Manchester.

His employer meets the costs of selling his old house, purchasing the new house and the costs of transporting his belongings.

The move is completed within six months of Toby taking up his new role.

The total cost of the relocation assistance is £20,000, which comprises qualifying removal benefits and expenses.

The first £8,000 is tax free, but a tax liability arises in respect of the remaining £12,000, which must be reported on Toby's P11D.

66. Suggestion Scheme Awards

Many companies run suggestion scheme awards where employees are rewarded for suggestions that are of benefit to the company. Provided that the scheme operates within certain parameters, suggestion scheme awards can be made tax-free.

To qualify for the exemption, the suggestion scheme must be open to all employees or to all employees in a particular group (such as a department or location), the suggestion rewarded must relate to the business and the suggestion could not have reasonably been expected to have been made in the normal course of the employee's job or at a meeting held for the purpose of making suggestions.

The tax exemption recognises two types of award – encouragement awards and financial benefit awards.

An encouragement award is made for merit or special effort on the part of the employee. Encouragement awards can be made free of tax and National Insurance to a limit of £25.

A financial benefit award is one made in respect of a suggestion which relates to an improvement in efficiency or effectiveness, the company has decided to adopt the suggestion and there is a reasonable expectation that its implementation will lead to financial benefit.

Financial benefit awards are exempt to the greater of 50% of the financial benefit expected in the first year after adoption or 10% of the benefit in the first five years after adoption, subject to an overall limit of £5,000.

Suggestion scheme awards that do not meet the conditions for exemption or are made in excess of the exempt limits are taxable.

Suggestion Scheme Awards

EFG Ltd runs a suggestion scheme to encourage employees to put forward ideas to improve the company.

An employee, Ruth, proposes a suggestion for changing the cups used for tea and coffee which generates savings of £3,000 in the first year and £2,000 a year thereafter. The suggestion is adopted and Ruth is given an award of £1,000.

The award is a financial benefit award. The exemption is capped at the higher of 50% of savings in first year (£1,500) or 10% of the savings in the first five years (£1,100), subject to an overall limit of £5,000.

The award made to Ruth is within the permitted maximum and can be made tax-free.

67. Long-Service Awards

In days gone by when it was more usual to have a job for life, employees were often given a gold watch or other memento to mark, say, 25 years of service.

The existence of a tax exemption enables employers to mark long service by making a tax-free award to the employee.

For the purposes of the exemption, a long-service award is one that is made to reward at least 20 years of service. To qualify for exemption the award must be in a non-cash form and no award must have been made in the previous ten years. The value of the exemption is capped at £50 per year of service.

Where the value of the award exceeds £50 a year, the excess is taxable. Cash awards are taxable in full.

Long-Service Awards

To mark 25 years' service with his employer, Albert is presented with a gold watch with a value of £1,000.

The award is exempt from tax.

68. Work-Related Training

The acquisition of additional skills is a valuable benefit. Where the training is work-related the provision is free of tax, regardless of whether the employer contracts with the training provider or whether the employee meets the costs initially and is reimbursed by the employer.

The definition of 'work-related training' is widely drawn and covers knowledge, skills and personal qualities that are likely to prove useful when performing the duties of a current or related employment or which will qualify or better qualify the employee to perform those duties or to participate in charitable or voluntary activities which are available to be performed in association with the employment. A related employment is one that the employee is to hold, has a serious opportunity of holding or can realistically expect to have a serious opportunity of holding in due course.

The exemption also covers associated travel expenses to the extent they would be deductible had the employee incurred them personally as well as the cost of books, training materials, etc.

The exemption does not apply to training unrelated to the job, which if provided constitutes a taxable benefit.

Work-Related Training

Ali has been promoted to a managerial role with his company. To equip him for the role, his employer sends him on a management training course.

The course constitutes work-related training and as such Ali is not taxed on its provision.

69. Additional Costs Of Working From Home

Technological advances have made it increasingly common for employees to work from home some or all of the time.

Working from home necessarily imposes additional costs on the employee, such as the cost of additional electricity used when working from home.

Where an employee is regularly required to work at home, the employer can pay the employee a tax-free allowance to cover the additional costs of working from home. The allowance is set at £4 per week for 2013/14. The tax-free rate is the same regardless of whether the employee works at home one day per week or five days per week.

HMRC may permit higher amounts to be paid tax-free if supported by evidence of actual expenditure. However, obtaining details of additional costs of working at home is unlikely to be cost- effective unless actual costs are considerably higher than the tax-free amount.

Additional Costs Of Working From Home

Sally's employer operates a hot-desking policy and every employee is required to work from home at least one day a week. As part of the homeworking arrangements Sally works from home every Wednesday. Her employer pays her an allowance of £4 per week, which is paid tax-free.

70. Homeworkers – Provision Of Supplies And Equipment

Where an employee works from home it is reasonable for the employer to provide the employee with the tools and equipment necessary for the employee to do his or her job. This may include, say, the provision of a computer, internet access, stationery and maybe a desk and office chair.

The provision of accommodation, supplies and services used by the employee in performing the duties of the employment is exempt from tax as long as any private use by the employee is insignificant. Where the provision is made other than on the employer's premises, such as in an employee's home, the exemption applies if the sole purpose of the provision is to enable the employee to perform the duties of the employment.

Homeworkers – Provision Of Supplies And Equipment

Bella regularly works from home and her employer provides her with a desktop computer and printer to enable her to do her job.

The computer is used predominantly for work purposes and any private use is incidental.

As the conditions for exemption are met, Bella is not taxed on the provision of the computer and printer.

71. Season Ticket Loans

The cost of commuting, especially into London by train, is significant and it is generally much cheaper for an employee to buy an annual season ticket than to buy a weekly or monthly ticket. To help employees meet the cost of an annual season ticket the employer may provide the employee with a season ticket loan.

Although a tax charge arises where an employee is provided with a cheap or interest-free loan by reason of his or her employment, an exemption exists for small loans. A small loan is a loan where the balance outstanding does not exceed £5,000 at any point in the tax year. If the employee has more than one small loan, the balances must be aggregated to check that this limit has not been exceeded.

The exemption limit for small loans is due to increase to £10,000 from 6 April 2014.

Family companies should be aware of the rules affecting loans to participators.

Season Ticket Loan

Billy commutes to work by train. A monthly ticket costs £450, whereas an annual season ticket costs £4,560.

Billy's employer agrees to provide him with an interest-free loan of £4,560 so that he can purchase an annual season ticket. The loan is repaid by means of a monthly deduction from his salary of £380.

The loan is less than £5,000 so the small exemption is in point and Billy is not taxed on the benefit of the interest-free loan.

By taking out the season ticket loan, Billy is able to save £70 a month on his travel costs.

72. Identifying The Elements Of The Termination Package

An employee may receive various different types of payment on the termination of his or her employment. Consequently, a typical termination package will include a number of elements, such as unpaid wages or salary, holiday pay, pay in lieu of notice, redundancy pay, *ex gratia* lump sums and non-cash benefits.

In taxing a termination package there is no one-size-fits-all policy. Different elements of the package will have different tax implications. Some elements are taxable as earnings, whereas others may be taxed as termination payments and are exempt to the extent that the £30,000 exemption (see Tip 74) remains available.

The key to taxing a termination package correctly is therefore to identify each individual element of the package and to tax that element correctly.

Identifying The Elements Of The Termination Package

Julian is made redundant and receives a payment of £10,000 on the termination of his employment. This comprises £5,000 in respect of unpaid salary, £1,000 in respect of accrued holiday and £4,000 in respect of statutory redundancy pay.

The salary payment and that in respect of accrued holiday are payments of earnings and are taxable in full. The statutory redundancy pay is exempt from tax but counts towards the £30,000 exemption for termination payments.

Chapter 6.
Termination Of Employment

73. Pay In Lieu Of Notice

Pay in lieu of notice (PILONs) often cause problems when dealing with termination payments and it is often thought (wrongly) that PILONs are tax-free to the extent that the £30,000 exemption (see Tip 74) remains available. To avoid falling into this trap it is important to look beyond the description and identify the true nature of the payment.

Where the contract of employment provides for payment to be made in lieu of the employee working his or her notice period (a contractual PILON), the payment is taxable in full as earnings and does not benefit from the £30,000 exemption. The same applies if it is customary to make a payment in lieu of notice, even if there is no express provision in the contract.

Another common scenario is that an employee is placed on gardening leave for the duration of the notice period. During this time the employee receives his usual salary or wages. This does not constitute a PILON and the payment of the wages or salary is taxable as a payment of earnings in the normal way.

However, where the employment is terminated without notice, any payment made for the failure to give proper notice is damages and the payment is made tax-free as a termination payment to the extent that the £30,000 threshold remains available.

Pay In Lieu Of Notice

Due to a downturn in business as a result of the recession, Barry's employment is terminated.

In his company it is customary for employees who are made redundant not to be required to work their notice period and to receive pay in lieu. However, there is no express for provision for payment in lieu of notice in the employment contract.

Despite the lack of contractual provision, the fact that it is customary for employees to receive pay in lieu of notice means that the payment is treated as earnings rather than damages and as such is taxable in full without the benefit of the £30,000 exemption.

74. The £30,000 Exemption

It is often wrongly assumed that the first £30,000 of any payment made on termination is tax free. However, the £30,000 exemption only applies to termination payments and benefits which are not otherwise taxable.

This means that payments of earnings such as wages and salary, accrued holiday and contractual and customary PILONs do not qualify and are taxable in full without the benefit of the exemption. However, the exemption does apply to redundancy pay (statutory and non-statutory), to compensation payments made for the loss of the job or the failure to give proper notice and *to ex gratia* lump sums.

The £30,000 exemption is only available once per termination.

The £30,000 Exemption

Ron is a senior manager in a large company. Following a restructure of the company's operations, he is made redundant. He is paid a termination payment of £200,000 comprising £50,000 in accrued salary, £100,000 in redundancy pay and an *ex gratia* payment of £50,000.

The payment of accrued salary is taxable in full as earnings.

The redundancy pay and *ex gratia* payments are termination payments of which the first £30,000 is tax-free. The balance above £30,000 (£120,000) is taxable.

75. Statutory Redundancy Pay

Statutory redundancy pay is payable to an employee who is made redundant after at least two years' continuous service.

The employee is entitled to 1.5 weeks' pay for each year of employment after their 41st birthday, 1 week's pay for each year of employment after their 22nd birthday up to their 41st birthday and half a week's pay for each year of employment up to their 22nd birthday.

Length of service is capped at 20 years for the purpose of calculating statutory redundancy pay and the maximum statutory redundancy pay payable is £13,500.

Statutory redundancy pay is paid tax-free but counts towards the £30,000 exemption.

Statutory Redundancy Pay

Janet is made redundant after 12 years' continuous employment with her employer. She is 55. Her weekly pay is £300 per week.

Janet has 12 years' service after her 41st birthday and is entitled to redundancy pay of 1.5 weeks per year of service. Therefore, she is entitled to 18 weeks' pay. This amounts to £5,400. She is paid this tax-free but it counts towards the £30,000 threshold, leaving £24,600 unused.

76. Outplacement Counselling

Where an employee's employment is terminated, the employer may provide the employee with advice and assistance to help the employee to come to terms with the loss of the job and to find a new job.

Provided that certain conditions are met, outplacement counselling can be provided free of tax. For the exemption to apply, each of the following conditions must be met.

1. The only or main purpose of providing the services is to enable the employee to adjust to the termination of employment or to find alternative employment.
2. The services provided must consist of giving advice or guidance, imparting or improving skills or providing or making available computer equipment or similar facilities.
3. The person to whom the services are provided must have been an employee throughout a period of two years up to the date when the services are provided or, if earlier, the date on which the employment was terminated.
4. The services must be made generally available to employees or a particular class of employees.

If outplacement counselling is provided and these conditions are not met, the employee is taxed in respect of the benefit of the counselling.

Outplacement Counselling

As a result of a fall in orders, PQR Ltd closes down one of its factories. All workers at the factory are made redundant.

To help them come to terms with the loss of their jobs and to find new employment, the company provides outplacement counselling for all employees who are made redundant. The terms of the exemption are met and the employees are not taxed on its provision.

Chapter 7.
Relief For Employment Expenses

77. Deduction For Employment Expenses
78. In The Performance Of The Duties
79. Wholly And Exclusively
80. Expense Must Be Necessarily Incurred
81. Nature Of Expense Not Amount
82. Reimbursed Expenses
83. Round-Sum Allowances
84. Travel Expenses
85. No Deduction For Ordinary Commuting
86. Special Rules For Temporary Workplaces
87. Fixed Term Appointments
88. Professional Membership Fees
89. Annual Subscriptions
90. Claiming a Deduction for Expenses

77. Deduction For Employment Expenses

Employees should claim a deduction for employment expenses that they incur wherever possible.

However, the rules that determine whether an employment expense is deductible are harsh and the tests are difficult to meet.

A deduction is only permitted in respect of an employment expense if the employee is obliged to incur and pay it as the holder of the employment and the amount is incurred wholly, necessarily and exclusively in the performance of the duties of the employment. These tests are strictly applied.

Special rules apply to govern the deductibility of certain expenses, such as travel expenses.

Deduction For Employment Expenses

David sells advertising space in a magazine. He is based at home. He is required to use his telephone in order to perform the duties of his employment.

He claims a deduction is respect of his business calls. The tests for deductibility are met and the deduction is permitted.

78. In The Performance Of The Duties

A distinction is drawn between expenses which put the employee in a position to perform the duties of the employment (for which no deduction is given) and those which are incurred *in* the performance of the duties (for which a deduction may be available if all the tests are met). The courts frequently make this distinction.

A working parent may need to incur childcare costs in order to be able to go to work. However, no deduction is permitted for these costs as they put the employee in the position to go to work, rather than being incurred in doing the job.

In a similar vein, the courts have disallowed journalists a deduction for the cost of newspapers as their job is writing copy and, while being abreast of news ensures that they are in a position to do their job, reading the newspapers is not part of the job.

It is for this reason that no relief is available for the costs of home to work travel.

In The Performance Of The Duties

Angela looks after her elderly mother. She employs a carer to look after her mother while she is at work as a hairdresser. She claims a deduction for the cost of the carer. The deduction is denied.

The expense is incurred to put Angela in a position where she can go to work; it is not incurred in the actual performance of her job as a hairdresser.

79. Wholly And Exclusively

A deduction is only given for an employment expense which is wholly and exclusively incurred in the performance of the duties of the employment. This requirement generally precludes a deduction from being given for expenses which serve a dual purpose.

An apportionment can be made where a definite part of the expense can be attributed wholly and exclusively to the duties of the employment. For example, an employee may use a mobile telephone for business and private calls. A deduction can be claimed in relation to the business calls. However, where the expense serves two purposes concurrently, such as the line rental of a landline used for both business and personal calls, an apportionment is not permitted.

Care must be taken only to claim a deduction for expenses that meet the wholly and exclusively test.

Wholly And Exclusively

Julia is required to look smart for work and buys office wear, which she only wears for work. She seeks a deduction for the cost of the clothes on the basis that they were bought solely for work.

The deduction is denied. The wholly and exclusively test is not met as the clothes also provide warmth and decency.

80. Expense Must Be Necessarily Incurred

Unlike the self-employed, employees are only allowed a deduction for expenses if the expense is necessarily incurred.

This is a harsh test to meet. The test is set by reference to the job rather than the individual holding it. To be deductible, the expense must be necessarily imposed on the employee by the duties of the employment. The fact that an expense is unavoidable does not in itself make that expense necessary. For the expense to be necessary it must be the case that the duties cannot be performed without incurring that expense.

Expense Must Be Necessarily Incurred

Hilda is required to attend an important meeting with a potential new customer. As she lives some distance from the office she spends the previous evening in a hotel to ensure that she is not late. She seeks a deduction for the cost of the hotel stay.

The deduction is denied. The expense is not necessary as it is not imposed by the job. It is Hilda's personal choice to live some distance from the office and to stay in the hotel overnight.

81. Nature Of Expense Not Amount

The tests as to whether an employment expense is deductible apply to the nature of the expense. They have no bearing on the amount that is deductible.

If the tests are met in relation to an expense, the deduction is given for the amount actually incurred. It does not matter whether there was a cheaper option.

Nature Of Expense Not Amount

As part of the duties of his employment, Alexander is required to attend a meeting in New York. He chooses to fly business class and claims a deduction for his travel expenses.

The tests for deductibility are met and the deduction is given. It does not matter that Alex could have travelled to New York more cheaply had he flown economy. The deduction is given for the business class ticket as that is the cost actually incurred.

82. Reimbursed Expenses

Unless a dispensation is in place (see Tip 95), where an employer reimburses expenses incurred by an employee in performing the duties of the employment, the employer must report the reimbursed expenses on the employee's P11D. The employee is then taxed on the reimbursed expense. To the extent that the expense is deductible, the onus is on the employee to claim a deduction to offset the tax charged on the reimbursement.

A deductible expense is not the same as an exempt one. Consequently, unless a dispensation is in force, it cannot be ignored and must be returned on the P11D.

Reimbursed Expenses

Holly is an accountant and is required to be a member of the ICAEW. She pays her annual subscription of £400 and reclaims the cost from her employer.

Her employer does not have a dispensation in force.

Holly's employer reports the reimbursed expense on her P11D.

Holly claims a deduction on her tax return to offset the tax liability that would otherwise arise.

83. Round Sum Allowances

Where employees are frequently required to incur expenses in the course of their jobs, it may seem easier from an administrative perspective to provide the employee with a round sum allowance from which to meet the expenses.

Where this approach is taken, it is important that it is dealt with correctly from a tax perspective to avoid falling foul of HMRC on a PAYE visit.

From a tax perspective, the whole amount of the allowance should be included in earnings for PAYE purposes and PAYE applied in the usual way. The onus is on the employee to claim a deduction for any deductible expenses met from the allowance.

For NIC purposes, any specific and distinct business expenses met from the allowance are ignored and the balance included in earnings for Class 1 NIC purposes.

The employer should ensure that systems are in place for employees to account for expenses met out of any round sum allowance provided.

Round Sum Allowances

Yvonne frequently incurs travel and other expenses as part of her job. Her employer provides her with a round sum allowance of £500 a month for the purposes of meeting the expenses. Yvonne is required to record details of her actual expenses and to provide receipts.

In one particular month, she incurs business expenses of £473.

The allowance of £500 is put through the payroll and subject to PAYE.

For National Insurance purposes, the business expenses are deducted from the allowance and the remaining £27 is treated as earnings on which Class 1 contributions are payable.

Yvonne must claim a deduction for the deductible expenses that she incurs to offset the tax paid on the round sum allowance.

84. Travel Expenses

Travel expenses do not need to meet the strict tests set out in Tip 77. The tests that determine deductibility of travel expenses are less stringent.

Employees are able to claim a deduction for:

1. travel in the performance of the duties;
2. travel for necessary attendance; and
3. travel between group employments.

Relief is also available for travel at the start and finish of an overseas employment and between employments where the duties are performed abroad.

No relief is available for travel which is ordinary commuting (see Tip 85).

Where the employer reimburses business expenses it is useful to apply for a dispensation to save work (see Tip 95). However, in the absence of a dispensation the employer must return details of the reimbursed expenses on the employee's P11D and the employee must claim a corresponding deduction to offset the tax liability that would otherwise arise.

Where travel expenses are deductible, there is no requirement that the employee travels by the cheapest method. The deduction is given for the costs actually incurred.

Travel Expenses

In her job as a buyer, Jenny is required to travel to various meetings with suppliers. She usually travels by train or taxi and claims back the cost of the travel from her employer.

Her employer does not have a dispensation in force so must return the reimbursed expenses on Jenny's P11D.

As the travel expenses are incurred in the performance of her duties, Jenny can claim a deduction for the expenses, which will offset the tax liability that would otherwise arise.

85. No Deduction For Ordinary Commuting

The general rule for the deductibility of expenses makes a distinction between expenses incurred to put someone in the position to do their job (non-deductible) and those incurred in doing the job.

The same principle applies to deny a deduction for the costs of home to work travel (generally referred to as ordinary commuting).

There are some limited exceptions to this rule where the employee travels to a temporary workplace or the duties are deemed to start from home, but these are the exception rather than the rule.

A deduction is also generally denied where an employee works from home but may be required to travel to the employer's office. The employee can have more than one workplace and, while the home may be a workplace it is also the home, so the journey remains a home to work journey rather than one between two workplaces.

A deduction is also denied for a journey which is virtually the same as the employee's ordinary commute.

See Tips 16, 46 and 49 for limited circumstances where it is possible for the employer to meet the costs of the employee's home to work travel without triggering a tax liability.

No Deduction For Ordinary Commuting

Grace works in an office in the town centre. She is required to attend a meeting at a client based in the next street. She travels from home to the meeting.

No deduction is permitted in respect of her travelling costs as the journey is virtually identical to her normal journey to work (substantially ordinary commuting).

86. Special Rules For Temporary Workplaces

The normal prohibition preventing a deduction for the costs of ordinary commuting does not apply where the employee is required to attend a temporary workplace for a limited duration.

A temporary workplace is one that an employee attends for the purposes of performing a task of limited duration or for some other temporary purpose.

The advantage of a temporary workplace is that the costs of travel from home to that temporary workplace are deductible.

However, a workplace is not a temporary workplace if the employee's attendance at that workplace is in the course of a period of continuous work lasting more than 24 months.

Temporary Workplace

Simon normally works in his firm's Northampton Office. He is seconded to work in the Leicester office for a period of 18 months after which he returns to the Northampton office.

The Leicester office is a temporary workplace which he attends for a limited duration of less than 24 months. He is therefore able to claim a deduction for the costs of travel from home to the Leicester office.

87. Fixed Term Appointments

The special rules that apply to allow a deduction for home to work travel where an employee attends a temporary workplace (see Tip 86) do not apply in the case of fixed term appointments, even if the appointment is for less than 24 months.

A workplace is not regarded as a temporary workplace if the employee attends that place for almost all of the period for which the employee holds that appointment.

Fixed Term Appointments

Bella is recruited on a 12-month contract to cover maternity leave. The contract is based at the company's office in Exeter.

Although the contract is for less than 24 months, the temporary workplace rules do not apply. The appointment is a fixed term appointment and Bella is based in the same place for the duration of the employment.

The workplace is not a temporary workplace and no deduction is available for the costs of home to work travel.

88. Professional Membership Fees

An employee is entitled to claim a deduction for the amount paid by way of a professional fee if the duties of the employment involve the practice of the profession to which the fee relates and registration, certification, licensing or other matter in respect of which the fee is payable is a condition, or one of the conditions, which must be met if the profession is to be practised in the performance of the duties.

The legislation (ITEPA 2003, s 343) lists the professional fees in respect of which a deduction is permitted.

Professional Membership Fees

Katy is employed as a chiropractor.

In order to practise she must maintain an entry in the Register of Chiropractors. She claims a deduction in respect of the associated fee.

89. Annual Subscriptions

An employee is also allowed to claim a deduction in respect of an annual subscription to a body which is approved by HMRC and the activities or objects of the body are of direct benefit or concern to the profession practised in the performance of the duties.

HMRC publish a list of approved bodies (List 3), which is available on the HMRC website (see www.hmrc.gov.uk/list3/index.htm).

Annual Subscriptions

Arthur is an electrical engineer and his employer requires that he is a member of the Institute of Electrical Engineers (IEE). He claims a deduction for his annual subscription, which is allowed by HMRC as membership is required as a condition of his employment and the IEE is an approved body.

90. Claiming a Deduction for Expenses

Where an employee incurs deductible expenses, it is important that the employee remembers to claim the deduction for those expenses, particularly if these have been reimbursed by the employer and there is no dispensation in force.

A deduction for expenses can be claimed on the employment pages of the self-assessment return where the employee is required to complete a self-assessment tax return or alternatively on form P87, which is available to download from the HMRC website at www.hmrc.gov.uk/forms/p87.pdf. Claims can also be made by letter and on form P810, which is available from HMRC.

The completed form should be returned to HMRC at the following address:

HM Revenue and Customs
Pay As You Earn
PO Box 1970
Liverpool
L75 1WX

Chapter 8.
Share Incentives

91. Share Incentive Schemes

Research shows that employees who own shares in the company for which they work are more productive and work harder.

To encourage employee share ownership tax incentives are available where shares or share options are offered under an approved scheme.

The share incentive plan (SIP) is an all-employee approved share scheme under which employers can allocate employees free shares worth up to £3,000. In addition, employees can buy up to £1,500 a year worth of additional shares from their pre-tax salary. These are known as partnership shares. Where the employee buys additional shares the employer can give further free shares of up to two free shares for each partnership share bought by the employee. These are known as matching shares. Dividends on plan shares can be invested to buy further shares (dividend shares).

The scheme must be approved by HMRC and the associated conditions met.

As long as the approval conditions are met no tax or NIC arises on the award of plan shares. Partnership shares are purchased out of pre-tax and pre-NIC salary. No tax charge arises on dividends reinvested as plan shares as long as they remain in the plan for three years. Further, no tax or NIC arises when the shares cease to be subject to the plan as long as they have been in the plan for three years.

Setting up a share incentive plan allows employees to acquire shares in the company in which they work in a tax-advantaged manner.

92. SAYE Share Option Schemes

A Save As You Earn (SAYE) Share Option Scheme is an approved share option scheme in which employees enter into a savings contract for three or five years. Under the contract the employee saves between £5 and £250 per month. The employee is granted an option to buy shares when the savings contract matures. The option price is fixed at the date of grant and can be up to 20% less than the market price of the shares at the time of grant.

SAYE Share Option Schemes are approved schemes and must meet a number of conditions for approval. Tax advantages are given in return for approval and the employee pays no income or capital gains tax on the grant or exercise of the options or on any repayment of the savings contract.

The employee is under no obligation to exercise the options and if it is not beneficial to do so, for example because the option price is higher than the current market value, the savings can be repaid to the employee when the contract matures.

The scheme must be available to all employees who wish to participate. It is a good way to encourage employees to consider buying shares in the company as it offers the opportunity to make a tax-free gain if the market value at exercise is higher than the option price, but is risk free as the employee can take the savings if preferred.

93. Company Share Option Plans

A company share option plan (CSOP) is an HMRC-approved discretionary share option plan. Conditions must be met in order to gain HMRC approval and tax advantages are granted in return for approval.

The discretionary nature of CSOP schemes makes them an attractive proposition for rewarding senior employees as they are not subject to the all-employee condition to which SIP and SAYE Share Option Schemes must adhere. However, unlike SAYE Share Option Schemes the option price must not be manifestly less than the market value at the date of grant; the opportunity to make a profit is reduced.

As long as the approval conditions are met, no income or capital gains tax is payable on grant or on exercise, as long as the options have been held for at least three years. However, capital gains tax may be payable on any gain on disposal if the shares are sold after exercise.

94. Unapproved Share Option Schemes

Although unapproved share option schemes lack the tax advantages available under approved schemes, they offer advantages in terms of flexibility and a reduced administrative burden which can make them attractive.

In particular, unapproved schemes are useful where employers do not want to be bound by the constraints of an approved scheme and want the flexibility to reward certain groups of employees.

Although a tax and National Insurance liability will arise on any gain on exercise, the liability will normally be met through the sale of some shares. To reduce the cost to the employer, the employer and employee can agree either that the employee will meet any secondary Class 1 National Insurance liability arising or for that liability to be transferred to the employee.

Chapter 9.
Compliance Issues And Saving Work

95. Dispensations
96. PAYE Settlement Agreements
97. RTI – 'On Or Before' Requirement
98. Pay PAYE On Time To Avoid Penalties
99. Quarterly Payment Of PAYE
100. Consider Basic PAYE Tools
101. File Correct P11Ds On Time

95. Dispensations

A dispensation is a notice from HMRC which removes the requirement for an employer to report certain expenses and benefits on an employee's P11D at the end of the year. It also saves employees the hassle of having to claim a deduction for business expenses reported on the P11D.

As noted in Tip 82, if a dispensation is not in place and an employer reimburses business expenses incurred by the employee, the employer must report the reimbursed expense on the P11D and the employee must claim a corresponding deduction to offset the tax liability that would otherwise arise. A dispensation removes the need to do this.

A dispensation can be granted in respect of items that are fully deductible and where the net result is that no tax is payable. Expenses typically included within a dispensation include travel costs, fuel for business travel company cars, business telephone calls, fees and subscriptions and business entertaining expenses.

Details of how to apply for a dispensation can be found on the HMRC website at:
www.hmrc.gov.uk/payerti/exb/schemes/dispensation.htm.

Dispensations

Employees of MNO Ltd regularly travel on business and reclaim their travel expenses from their employer.

To save work, the employer agrees a dispensation with HMRC. This relieves the employer of the need to report the reimbursed expenses on the employees' P11Ds and for the employees to claim the corresponding deduction.

Work is saved all round.

96. PAYE Settlement Agreements

A PAYE Settlement Agreement (PSA) enables the employer to settle the tax and National Insurance liability on certain benefits and expenses on their employees' behalf.

A PSA can be used for expenses that are difficult to manage under the normal reporting rules. To qualify for inclusion within a PSA the item in question must be minor in amount, paid irregularly or be an item in respect of which it is impracticable to operate PAYE or to determine the value to be included on the employee's P11D. By contrast, a PSA cannot be used for cash payments, large benefits provided regularly, such as company cars, shares, items on which PAYE has already been deducted or which are reflected in the employee's tax code or motor mileage profit under the AMAP scheme.

A PSA must be agreed with HMRC no later than 6 July after the end of the tax year to which it relates. The employer pays tax on the grossed up value of the benefits included within the PSA. Class 1B National Insurance contributions are payable in place of the Class 1 or Class 1A liability that would otherwise arise.

The tax and National Insurance due under the PSA is payable in a single instalment by 22 October after the tax year where payment is made electronically or by 19 October otherwise.

PAYE Settlement Agreements

DEF Ltd holds a Christmas party for employees each year.

The party is a lavish affair and costs £175 per head. As the exemption for Christmas parties (see Tip 63) is not in point, the employer agrees to settle the liability by means of a PSA so that the employees do not suffer a tax bill in respect of the party.

97. RTI – 'On Or Before' Requirement

Under Real Time Information (RTI) employers are required to report to HMRC electronically details of pay and deductions 'on or before' the time at which payment is made to the employee.

HMRC recognise that the requirement to report at or before making the payment to the employee could cause difficulties in some cases, for example where payments are made to employees weekly but the employer only runs the payroll each month. To allow small employers time to adjust, the 'at or before' requirement is relaxed for employers with fewer than 50 employees until 5 April 2014. Under the relaxation small employers can report pay and deductions to HMRC when they run the payroll as long as the report is made before the end of the tax month in which the payment is made to the employee.

However, it is recommended that small employers adopt automated systems that allow the 'at or before' requirement to be met so that they do not suffer unnecessary penalties once automated penalties are introduced.

RTI – 'On Or Before' Requirement

Mark is a small employer with ten employees.

He pays five employees weekly every Friday and the remaining five employees monthly on the 28th of the month.

He runs his payroll once a month at the end of the month and submits a single RTI report to HMRC.

Under the relaxation for small employers this is fine until 5 April 2014.

However, from that date Mark will need to file pay and deductions details every time he pays employees and will need to make weekly submissions at or before paying his weekly paid employees as well as a submission when paying monthly paid employees.

98. Pay PAYE On Time To Avoid Penalties

Penalties are charged if employers fail to pay PAYE on time and in full on more than one occasion in the tax year. The penalty depends on how much is paid late and the number of defaults in the tax year. The first late payment is not counted as a default.

The penalty rates are as follows:

Number Of Defaults In Tax Year	Penalty Percentage
1–3	1%
4–6	2%
7–9	3%
10 or more	4%

The percentage is applied to the amount that is paid late in the tax year (ignoring the first late payment in the year).

It is important that good systems are in place to ensure PAYE is paid on time every month. Where payment is made electronically cleared funds must reach HMRC's account by 22nd of the month. Where payment is made by cheque this must reach HMRC by 19th of the month.

Care should be taken where the due date falls on a weekend or bank holiday and extra time should be allowed to ensure that the payment is not accidently made late as this could prove costly. In such cases payment must reach HMRC or funds clear, as appropriate, by the last banking day before the due date.

Pay PAYE On Time To Avoid Penalties

OPQ Ltd has a monthly PAYE and NIC bill of £5,000. In the 2013/14 tax year it pays late on three occasions.

The first late payment is ignored meaning that there are two defaults in the year.

The total PAYE paid late (ignoring the first late payment) is £10,000.

The penalty rate for two defaults is 1%. The company suffers a late payment penalty of £100 as a result of the late payments.

This could have been avoided by making payments on time.

99. Quarterly Payment Of PAYE

Employers whose average PAYE and NIC bill does not exceed £1,500 per month can choose to pay their PAYE quarterly rather than monthly. Not only does this save work, it also provides the company with a cashflow benefit.

A further advantage is that the company only needs to make a payment to HMRC on four occasions in the tax year, which reduces the scope to pay late and trigger a late payment penalty.

100. Consider Basic PAYE Tools

All employers (with only a very few limited exceptions) must report PAYE in real time by October 2013.

Although there are numerous commercial payroll products on the market, small employers with nine or fewer employees can use HMRC's free payroll software product, 'Basic PAYE Tools', to work out their PAYE and NIC and to meet their RTI filing requirements.

Basic PAYE Tools is available to download from the HMRC website at www.hmrc.gov.uk/payerti/payroll/bpt/paye-tools.htm.

101. File Correct P11Ds On Time

Where employers provide taxable non-cash benefits and expenses to employees they must provide details of those expenses and benefits to HMRC on form P11D (for employees earning at a rate of at least £8,500 a year and directors) or on form P9D (for employees with an earnings rate of less than £8,500 a year) no later than 6 July after the end of the tax year to which they relate. A statutory Class 1A return and employer's declaration (form P11D(b)) must be filed by the same date.

There is no requirement to file electronically, but most employers find it easier to do so. This can be done using either HMRC's new Expenses and Benefits Online service (see www.hmrc.gov.uk/forms/online-exb.pdf) or by using HMRC's PAYE Online Service or a commercial software package with online filing capabilities.

It is important that care is taken to ensure the returns are correct, and penalties for incorrect returns can be high (up to £3,000 per incorrect return). Penalties may also be charged if the returns are filed late.

www.ingramcontent.com/pod-product-compliance
Ingram Content Group UK Ltd.
Pitfield, Milton Keynes, MK11 3LW, UK
UKHW020627120926
15112UKWH00034B/82

9 780957 613942